Raoul Wallenberg

*Rescuing Thousands
from the Nazis' Grasp*

Debra McArthur

Enslow Publishers, Inc.

40 Industrial Road	PO Box 38
Box 398	Aldershot
Berkeley Heights, NJ 07922	Hants GU12 6BP
USA	UK

http://www.enslow.com

This book is dedicated with sincere thanks to:
Kate and Eugene Lebovitz, survivors
and
Ms. Fran Sternberg of the Midwest Center
for Holocaust Education
May we never forget the struggles of those who were persecuted
and of those who sacrificed so much for the sake of others.

Copyright © 2005 by Debra McArthur

Library of Congress Cataloging-in-Publication Data:

McArthur, Debra.
    Raoul Wallenberg : rescuing thousands from the Nazis' grasp /
Debra McArthur.
        p. cm. — (Holocaust heroes and Nazi criminals)
    Includes bibliographical references and index.
    ISBN 0-7660-2530-6
     1. Wallenberg, Raoul, 1912–1947. 2. Righteous Gentiles in the Holocaust.
3. Holocaust, Jewish (1939–1945)—Hungary. 4. World War,
1939–1945—Jews—Rescue—Hungary. 5. Righteous Gentiles—Sweden—Biography.
6. Ambassadors—Sweden—Biography. I. Title. II. Series.
    D804.66.W35M33 2005
    940.53'1835'092—dc22

                   2004016153

To Our Readers: We have done our best to make sure all Internet Addresses in this book were
active and appropriate when we went to press. However, the author and the publisher have no
control over and assume no liability for the material available on those Internet sites or on
other Web sites they may link to. Any comments or suggestions can be sent by e-mail to
comments@enslow.com or to the address on the back cover.

Illustration Credits: Enslow Publishers, Inc, p. 40; National Archives and Records
Administration, pp. 5, 26, 38, 47, 59, 73, 88, 106, 134 (third from top), 137 (third from top);
Reproduced from the Collections of the Library of Congress, p. 98; USHMM, pp. 44, 134 (second
from bottom), 135 (top), 137 (second from bottom); USHMM, courtesy of Amira Kohn-Trattner,
p. 43; USHMM, courtesy of Eva Hevesi Ehrlich, p. 65; USHMM, courtesy of Hagstromer &
Qviberg Fondkommission, pp. 3, 4, 8, 11, 134 (top), 139, 152, 155, 157, 158; USHMM, Courtesy
of the Israel Government Press Office, pp. 22, 25; USHMM, Courtesy of Lena Kurtz Deutsch, p.
33; USHMM, courtesy of Lorenz Schmuhl, pp. 125, 134 (third from bottom), 136 (top), 137 (third
from bottom), 138 (top); USHMM, courtesy of the Main Commission for the Persecution of the
Crimes Against the Polish Nation, pp. 134 (second from top), 136 (bottom), 137 (second from top),
138 (bottom); USHMM, courtesy of the National Archives and Records Administration, pp. 80,
129; USHMM, courtesy of the National Museum of American Jewish History, pp. 134 (bottom),
135 (bottom), 137 (bottom); USHMM, courtesy of Per and Ellena Anger, pp. 34, 52; USHMM,
courtesy of Randolph Braham, p. 101; USHMM, courtesy of Thomas Veres, pp. 82, 111.

Cover Illustration: USHMM, courtesy of Hagstromer & Qviberg Fondkommission; USHMM,
courtesy of Lorenz Schmuhl (background).

Contents

Fast Facts About Raoul Wallenberg

Name: Raoul Gustav Wallenberg
Born: August 4, 1912, Kapptsta, Sweden (near Stockholm)
Family:
  Father—Raoul Oscar Wallenberg (died May 1912)
  Mother—Maj Wising Wallenberg von Dardel (died 1979)
  Stepfather—Fredrik von Dardel (died 1979)
  Half-sister—Nina von Dardel Lagergren
  Half-brother—Guy von Dardel
Education: University of Michigan (Ann Arbor, Michigan, United States); Bachelor of Arts, Architecture
Jobs held:
  Sales, South African Export Import Co.; Capetown, South Africa (1935)
  Banker, Holland Bank; Haifa, Israel (1936)
  Investor and sales, various small business interests; Europe (1937–1941)
  International sales, import/export specialty foods; Europe (1942–1944)
  Secretary, Swedish Legation; Budapest, Hungary (1944–1945)
Death: Date unknown. Reported as July 17, 1947, Lubyanka Prison, Soviet Union. Cause unknown. Reported as heart attack, possible murder or execution.
Last seen: January 17, 1945, leaving Budapest with Soviet military escort. Reported sightings in Soviet prisons 1945–1978(?)
Notable for: Rescue efforts in Budapest, Hungary, in cooperation with Swedish legation, funded by War Refugee Board and Jewish Joint Distribution Committee.
Saved the lives of thousands of Hungarian Jews from the Nazis. Estimated lives saved: at least twenty thousand; possibly as many as one hundred thousand.

1

Daring Rescue

In the cold dawn on November 23, 1944, at the Hegyeshalom train station on the border of Austria and Hungary, three thousand Hungarian Jewish prisoners waited. Hundreds of men, women, and children were already crowded into locked cattle cars of the train. Many more stood on the platform, waiting to be ordered into the remaining cars. Their next stop would be a Nazi concentration camp. The prisoners had been forced to walk 125 miles from Budapest to the train station with little clothing to protect them from the cold Hungarian winter. Few had shoes. They had seen guards shoot dozens, perhaps hundreds, of the elderly and weak who could not keep up; bodies of the dead were left alongside the road. The prisoners were miserable with the infestation of lice. Many had given up all hope of surviving.

A report filed by a group of Swiss diplomats who witnessed the scene described the prisoners who waited on the platform as being, in the worst state of demoralization imaginable . . . [T]he endless ordeal of the marches, the almost complete lack of nourishment, the constant dread that in Germany they were to be taken to annihilation in the gas chambers, have brought about such a condition . . . that they no longer possess human shape and lack all human dignity.[1]

German Schutzstaffel (SS) soldiers, Hungarian gendarmes, and members of Hungary's own Nazi group, the Arrow Cross, separated the prisoners into groups of one hundred. The German officers would need an accurate count of the prisoners transported that day. Groups of eighty people would be loaded into each train car. The hundreds of people already in the cattle cars were so tightly packed that they could not sit down. Each train car of prisoners had one bucket of water and one bucket to be used for a toilet. There was no food for the trip, which would take several days.

Suddenly, a line of automobiles and trucks marked with the blue and gold colors of Sweden appeared out of the darkness and parked next to the platform. Swedish diplomat Raoul Wallenberg emerged from the first car. He began shouting, "In the name of the Szálasi government, I demand those with Swedish passports to raise them high!"[2] Wallenberg, in his long raincoat and wide-brimmed hat, swept onto the train platform, demanding that the Arrow Cross guards release those prisoners with Swedish protective passes.[3]

Wallenberg's diplomatic mission was to save as many Hungarian Jews from the Nazis as he could, but he had almost arrived too late. In the months before he began his work, over four hundred thousand Jews had been deported from the country provinces of Hungary. Some were working in labor groups, but most had been sent to death camps.[4] When Wallenberg arrived in Hungary in July 1944, the last remaining

Jewish population was in the city of Budapest. If the Nazis succeeded, those Jews would also soon be murdered and all the Jews of Hungary would be dead. Wallenberg was determined to prevent that.

Since July, Wallenberg had been printing and giving out Swedish protective passes called Schutz-passes. A Schutz-pass granted the protection of the Swedish government to the person named on it. The pass implied that person had plans to emigrate to Sweden, but that would be impossible during the war.[5] Bearers of Schutz-passes were not to be deported or sent to Nazi concentration camps. That day on the platform, Wallenberg brought more Schutz-passes with him, but not nearly enough to save the thousands of Jews being loaded into the cattle cars.

Several Arrow Cross soldiers stepped forward to confront Wallenberg. They lowered their rifles until the bayonets rested on Wallenberg's chest. Wallenberg refused to be intimidated. He ran around to the other side of the train and climbed on top of one of the train cars. Through the air vents he shouted, "Are there any Swedish-protected Jews in there who've lost their passes?"[6] Voices from within the car shouted, "Yes!" and Wallenberg ran along the top of the train cars, sliding Schutz-passes through the air vents to the waiting hands of deportees below.

German soldiers shouted at him to get down. Arrow Cross guards fired over his head, but none hit him. Wallenberg finally jumped down from the train and left the platform. A few minutes later, he returned with a Hungarian police officer and armed Hungarian soldiers whom he had bribed with rum and cigarettes. With this new show of force, the Arrow Cross soldiers opened the sealed cattle cars and

Above is a passport photo of Raoul Wallenberg.

stepped back. Wallenberg called out for all who had passes to come out of the train and get into the waiting trucks.[7]

Wallenberg was not finished. Next, he demanded the guards release all other Jews who had lost their passes, as well as those who had applied for passes but were captured before they could pick them up at the Swedish legation office. When the German soldiers insisted that Wallenberg must have a list of those Jews, he brought out a large, leather-bound book. As he called out common Jewish names, people answered. Some actually heard their names, but many others understood Wallenberg's trick. He did not know any of them, but none of the soldiers knew that, and no one could verify their identities. As the prisoners stepped forward, each gave his or her full name, and Wallenberg's assistant wrote the names in the book and on blank passes.[8]

As he walked through the crowd, Wallenberg spoke to the people, pretending to recognize some. "So here you are," he said to one, "We had to bring it to you." To another, "Sorry you couldn't make it to the legation on time."[9] He scolded the Arrow Cross guards as well. "See, I have a pass for this man, and you took him away before I could give it to him."[10]

As those Jews left the platform to get into the trucks, Wallenberg gave one last chance to those who remained. "Which of you has recently lost your Swedish pass?" he asked. "Raise your hands." Joni Moser, Wallenberg's eighteen-year-old assistant, went among the Jews, whispering, "Raise your hands! Raise your hands!" Many did, and Wallenberg walked among them, touching some raised hands and instructing them to go to the cars. He apologized to those he could not help. "I am sorry. I am trying to take the youngest ones first. I want to save a nation."[11] Miriam Herzog heard Wallenberg use this expression the day he saved her life, and it surprised her. "I had never heard of the idea of a Jewish nation before," she said. "Jewish people, of course, but not a Jewish nation."[12]

Wallenberg saved three hundred people from certain death that morning at Hegyeshalom. Probably fewer than thirty of them had ever originally had a Schutz-pass. Those taken from the train that day were driven back to the Swedish-protected houses in Budapest.

Incidents like this one became legend among the Jews in Budapest. Per Anger, a Swedish diplomat who worked with Wallenberg during this time said, "It was through these acts that the rumor was spread of his almost superhuman ability, in seemly hopeless situations, to snatch victims from the Nazi executioners. He became hated but feared by the Arrow Cross men. He became the Budapest Jews' hope of rescue from the final liquidation."[13]

Raoul Wallenberg was never required to take on the dangerous work he chose. This work, however, gave purpose and meaning to the life of a man raised in the luxury of a wealthy Swedish family. He desperately wanted to save the Jewish nation from being murdered out of existence and found great satisfaction in his efforts. According to Joni Moser, "It is not given to many men to live such a life, equipped with the spark of initiative, an irresistible personal radiance, and a tireless energy, and with these to be able to save thousands of one's fellow-men."[14]

He could not save all of the Hungarian Jews, but he could, and did, save thousands.

2

Unlikely Hero

Raoul Gustav Wallenberg was born August 4, 1912, and was named for the father he never knew—the father who died of cancer three months before Raoul was born. Raoul and his mother, Maj Wising Wallenberg, lived in the house of Maj's widowed mother, where the two women doted on the little boy. Six years later, Maj married Fredrik von Dardel. Maj and Fredrik later had two more children, but those early years of tenderness with his mother and grandmother shaped Raoul's personality. According to Raoul's half sister, Nina, Raoul "gave and received so much love that he grew up to be an unusually generous, loving, and compassionate person."[1]

The Education of a Wallenberg

For generations, the Wallenbergs had been one of the most influential families in Swedish banking and business. André Wallenberg founded the Stockholm Enskilda Bank in 1856. He was an entrepreneur who financed new companies and made international banking and business deals. André Wallenberg fathered twenty children, among them successful international businessmen, bankers, and diplomats. His youngest son, Marcus, later took over the management of the bank and made investments in international industries that created a financial empire.

Raoul's grandfather, Gustav Wallenberg, was determined that young Raoul have all the advantages that a Wallenberg should have, so he took charge of Raoul's education. After Raoul finished high school and a brief period in the Swedish army, his grandfather sent him to live in France for several months to improve his French, even though Raoul already knew English, German, and Russian languages. His grandfather was determined that Raoul would someday be the head of an international bank.

Raoul, however, had a talent for drawing, and he had always been fascinated by building design. His grandfather agreed to allow Raoul to study architecture before he began his study of banking, and he gave him the money to travel to America in 1931 to study architecture at the University of Michigan in Ann Arbor. Raoul Wallenberg did well in his studies and graduated in 1935, receiving a medal for outstanding work from the American Institute of Architects.

During his college years, Wallenberg traveled across the United States, Canada, and Mexico. Gustav Wallenberg provided the money for these trips, intending them as an opportunity for his grandson to learn more about people of different cultures and backgrounds. Raoul often wrote letters about his experiences, thanking his grandfather for his support and telling him about his adventures. Gustav Wallenberg shared these letters with others and was concerned that they might get the idea that Raoul was having too much fun, instead of taking his education seriously. In a letter, his grandfather wrote, "The fact that you've had a good time is of secondary importance and should be downplayed. One should not seek enjoyment in these serious times, and if one does one should not talk about it."[2]

After Raoul Wallenberg left architecture school, his grandfather arranged for him to begin his business education. He asked his friend Albert Floren to give Raoul an unpaid position in the South African office of Floren's Swedish-South Africa Export Import Company. Although he did not care for the job very much, Raoul did learn a great deal about business. After six months there, Raoul returned to visit his grandfather, who then sent him to pursue the next part of his education: banking.

Battling Anti-Semitism

In 1936, Raoul's grandfather arranged another unpaid job for him, this time with the Holland Bank in the Palestinian city of Haifa. Many of his fellow workers were Jews who had escaped from Hitler's Germany. They told of the persecution they suffered at the hands of the Hitler's Nazis.

In 1933, the Nazi party had taken control of Germany, whose democracy was weakened by a poor economy and political unrest. Soon afterward, Hitler began a propaganda campaign to destroy his political opponents and built a military force to arrest anyone who resisted him. Hitler did not target the Jews because of their religious beliefs, but because of their race. The Jewish race became a scapegoat upon which to blame all the ills of German society. This was Hitler's way of unifying the non-Jewish Aryan population. He identified the Jewish race as the enemy of the "pure" and superior Aryan race. Hitler's idea of an Aryan person, was a Northern European with fair hair. He began a propaganda campaign in which he claimed that the Jews were responsible for the poor state of the German economy. He used Darwin's theory of evolution to portray the Aryan race as superior and the Jewish race as being destined for extinction.

The Nazis enacted strict laws to confiscate businesses and property of the Jews, as well as excluding them from government jobs, public schools, and other areas of society. Jewish property was seized and distributed to Aryans, and Jewish jobs were given to Aryan citizens. Soon Germany was consumed by hatred for the Jews, called anti-Semitism. In 1935, laws were passed that even denied German citizenship to Jews. Thousands of German Jews tried to emigrate to other countries, but it was hard to find a place to go. There were Nazi supporters in nearly every country, even the United States. Opinion polls showed that nearly 20 percent of Americans saw the Jews as a threat to America.[3]

Anti-Semitism followed the Jews who went to Palestine, where Jewish Zionists hoped to establish a separate country for Jews. Nazi agents distributed newspapers and leaflets in Palestine to stir up hatred of the Jews, especially among the Arabs in the region. Some Arabs attacked Jewish businesses and farms. Raoul downplayed the danger in his letters to his grandfather. "There has been some bomb throwing, with meager results," he reported.[4]

Wallenberg's time in Haifa made him keenly aware of the persecution the Jews suffered. He was himself one-sixteenth Jewish, through the grandmother who had helped to raise him so lovingly in his early years. Her Jewish grandfather, Michael Benedicks, had settled in Sweden before 1800. He later became a member of the Lutheran Church and married a Christian woman.[5] Raoul Wallenberg was proud of this background, and sometimes even exaggerated his Jewish heritage.

He once told philosophy professor Ingemar Hedenius, "A person like me who is both a Wallenberg and half-Jewish, can never be defeated."[6]

Uncertain Future

While in Haifa, Raoul had the difficult task of telling his grandfather how he felt about the future Gustav Wallenberg had planned for him. "I may not be particularly suited for banking at all," he wrote Gustav in July 1936. "To tell you the truth, I don't find myself very bankerish . . . My temperament is better suited to some positive line of work than to sitting around saying no."[7] Raoul was frustrated by his employer and impatient that his grandfather kept arranging unpaid jobs.

Raoul left Haifa in July 1936 to return to Sweden to complete his military service. Afterward, he contacted many relatives and friends of his grandfather to find a job, but with no luck. In March 1937, Gustav Wallenberg died. Raoul was at last free to pursue other careers besides banking. Unfortunately, his American architecture degree did not qualify him for a position with architecture firms in Sweden. At age twenty-five, Raoul felt he was too old to begin working on another degree, but the Wallenberg name carried great expectation, and Raoul needed to establish himself in business somehow.

Over the next few years, Raoul became involved in several different business ventures. First, he went into business with an inventor who had patented a new zipper fastener, but he could not interest any buyers. Next, he tried to market a wine cork that would come out of the bottle without using a corkscrew, but the French wine makers were not interested. He tried selling both coffee and sardines, but again was not successful in his ventures.[8]

The World at War

By 1939, Hitler was ready to begin his move to dominate Europe. On September 1, 1939, Germany invaded Poland. Britain and France declared war on Germany, thus beginning World War II. The German forces were strong, however. They also found people in each country they conquered who were willing to join the drive to persecute the Jews. Even before the invasion of Poland, tens of thousands of people, including Jews, gypsies, homosexuals, and the mentally ill, had been sent to concentration camps in Germany.

Hitler's power in Europe quickly grew both stronger and more dangerous. By the end of 1940, The Germans controlled much of the continent, including Austria, Poland, Norway, Denmark, Belgium, France, and other areas. Jewish businesses in most of these countries had been closed. Jews in Poland had to wear badges identifying themselves. Hitler had finished a new concentration camp at Auschwitz, Poland. Thousands of people were transported there. Their fate was unknown.

A New Career

In the midst of all this, Wallenberg was still seeking to establish himself in business. In the fall of 1941, Wallenberg met Koloman Lauer, a Jewish businessman in Stockholm, Sweden, who imported and exported specialty food items. Lauer was looking for a Gentile (non-Jewish person) who could travel freely throughout Nazi-occupied Europe to sell his products. Wallenberg, with his knowledge of languages, travel experience, and business background, was perfect for the job.

Wallenberg started his new job in January 1942. He began his travels with a trip to France, which had been controlled by the Germans since June 1940. The Nazis had already captured thousands of French people and sent them to detention camps where many died of starvation and disease. Others were sent to Auschwitz. In Paris, Jewish property was sold and the money taken by the Nazis. Soldiers went door-to-door to take prisoners. Jewish communities were heavily taxed. Jewish temples were attacked.

Lauer's import/export business put Wallenberg in a position to deal with many types of people. He worked with Jewish business contacts of Lauer's, French Gentiles, and with Nazi government officials in order to sell Lauer's products. Through his business for Lauer, Wallenberg saw firsthand the suffering of the victims of the Nazi regime. That winter, he took his sister, Nina, to see an American movie called *Pimpernel Smith*. Originally a Hungarian Jew, British film star Leslie Howard played a lovable but bumbling university professor who cleverly managed to outwit Nazis and save Jews. Afterward, Raoul told Nina he wanted to be like that professor.[9]

Wallenberg's business dealings for the next eighteen months took him to many parts of Europe. He made business calls in Berlin, Germany, and Switzerland. Wallenberg's work for Lauer also took him to Hungary. Lauer had family as well as business contacts there. Wallenberg traveled twice to Budapest, Hungary, to conduct business. Lauer ask him to check on the well-being of Mrs. Lauer's family in Budapest. Although Hungary was still free, it was allied with Germany. Anti-Jewish laws were passed, forbidding Jewish people from working in government jobs and forcing some Jewish businesses to close. Still, some business owners bribed Gentile friends into running their stores so the Jews could keep ownership. They raised money to support the poorer members of their community. Although the Hungarian Jews had heard the stories of Adolf Hitler's atrocities, they did not think their Hungarian leaders would allow them to be Hitler's next victims.

Hitler's "Final Solution" to the "Jewish Problem"

Hitler often described what to do with the Jews as the "Jewish question" or "Jewish problem." On January 20, 1942, a group of Nazi leaders sat down in Berlin to discuss this. At what became known as the Wannsee Conference, they developed what they called a "final solution." It was there that they planned to deport the Jews, force some of them to work, and eventually kill them all.

During the summer of 1942, newspapers in Europe and the United States published reports of the mass murder of Polish Jews. Many people thought the stories were exaggerated; they believed such a thing was not possible. In August 1942, Dr. Gerhart Reigner of the World Jewish Congress sent a telegram from Geneva, Switzerland, to both New York and London that Hitler intended to kill all the Jews in Europe.[10] Soon afterward, a Catholic humanitarian who adopted the pseudonym "Jan Karski" entered a death camp disguised as a guard and witnessed mass executions there. He reported it to both British and American authorities, but they took no action.[11]

At first, Hitler's soldiers executed Jews by firing squad. In most cases, Jews were ordered to dig long trenches. Then they were stripped of all their clothing and lined up next to the trenches. Men, women, and children were then killed by firing squads. Their bodies fell into the trenches they had dug. This method of execution was difficult for even the most brutal Nazi soldiers. Many of them drank too much, and some even had breakdowns and turned their guns against their own officers.[12] When SS Commander Heinrich Himmler toured one camp, the commander in charge, General Erich von dem

Bach-Zelewski, showed him how demoralized the troops were. "Observe how shattered they are," he told Himmler. "These men's nerves are ruined for the rest of their lives."[13] They decided that they needed to find a better method of carrying out Hitler's final solution.

By 1942, the Germans had experimented with several kinds of gases to find an effective and efficient means of killing thousands of people in a short time. They discovered that the chemical Zyklon B would kill people very quickly. It could be stored in solid pellet form in cans but turned to a gas when exposed to air. Many people could be packed into a sealed room to be gassed all at once. According to Dr. Hans Munch, an SS physician at Auschwitz, the gas containers were dropped into air vents from the top of the gas chambers. He explained:

> Zyklon B began to work as soon as it was released from the canisters. The effects of the gas were observed through a peephole by an assigned doctor or the SS officer on duty. After three to five minutes, death could be certified, and the doors were opened as a sign that the corpses were cleared to be burned.[14]

The Invasion of Hungary

Defeat of the Germans in the war could allow the Allies to stop the slaughter of the Jews, but as the fighting continued, thousands of innocent people were being killed every day. In January 1944, United States President Franklin Delano Roosevelt established the War Refugee Board (WRB). Its goal was to save Jews and other groups from the Nazis.

By this time, the largest Jewish population remaining in central Europe was in Hungary. Hitler had ordered the Hungarian leaders to take care of the Jewish problem, but the Hungarians resisted. The Hungarian troops were fighting on the side of Germany, but the Germans had lost several key battles in late 1943. The Allies had taken control of several areas Germany had previously conquered. Italy had surrendered to the Allies and declared war on Germany. It was more and more likely that the Germans could lose the war, and Hungarian leaders did not want the Allies to hold them responsible for the deaths of hundreds of thousands of their own citizens.

After Hungarian troops suffered great losses in a battle with the Soviets, Hungary's Prime Minister Miklós Kállay and Regent Miklós Horthy wanted to make peace with the western Allies. They feared that their troops would be destroyed along with Germany's and that the Soviets would take over Hungary. They sent representatives to Italy and Turkey to negotiate with the British and Americans. Nazi agents learned of the plan, and German diplomat Edmund Veesenmayer sent a report to Hitler.[15] On March 19, German forces invaded Hungary. Kállay was forced to step down from his position as prime minister and was replaced by Döme Sztójay, the former Hungarian ambassador to Berlin. Veesenmayer was named plenipotentiary, a position that gave him power over German affairs in Hungary. Regent Horthy was allowed to retain his position, but his power would be limited by the new pro-Nazi government.[16]

Adolf Eichmann had already distinguished himself in Austria during the deportations of Jews. Hitler now sent him to Hungary to lead the drive to eliminate the Hungarian Jews. He was well-known among the Nazis for his determination to kill as many Jews as he could. Eichmann once told a friend, "I will jump into my grave laughing because the fact that I have the deaths of five million Jews on my conscience gives me extraordinary satisfaction."[17]

20

Eichmann wasted no time in beginning his plan to contain and control Jews in Hungary. Within two weeks of the German occupation, he demanded the formation of a Jewish Council. The council was a group of Jewish leaders who would deliver communication from the Nazi leaders to the people. Eichmann knew that he must avoid panic among the citizens. He would convince the Jewish Council that each new restriction was for the welfare and protection of their people.

Eichmann announced that Jewish workers were needed to work in factories to aid the German war effort. He also said that the adult workers would be more content if their families were allowed to go with them. The rural parts of Hungary were the easiest place to begin because the communities were somewhat isolated from each other, and many of the working-class people were less resistant to the anti-Semitic propaganda of the Nazis.

The German *sonderkommando*, Eichmann's special squad, began rounding up thousands of Jewish families from the countryside with the assistance of Hungarian military officers called *gendarmes*. The prisoners were sent into nearby towns where they were kept at temporary holding areas such as residential areas, factories, or even outdoor enclosures. They were to be held only until they could be sent to the work camps. As houses were vacated, Hungarian gendarmes went in and took everything of value left behind. These items were then sent to the Reich. In many cases, Gentile neighbors moved into the empty houses.

It was not easy to find people or organizations willing to help stop the persecution of the Jews. The newly-formed War Refugee Board could not send its people into Hungary, as the WRB represented the United States and the Allies. Because Hungary was now under German control, it was enemy

Adolf Eichmann

For Adolf Eichmann, Wallenberg was a threatening opponent in a contest both desperately wanted to win: the struggle for the Jews of Hungary.

Eichmann was born in Solingen, Germany in 1906. The family moved to Austria, where Eichmann later worked as a laborer and a traveling salesman. In 1932, he joined the Nazi Party in Austria. In 1938, he handled the forced emigration of Austrian Jews. He sent about one hundred fifty thousand Jews out of Austria in eighteen months. In 1944, Eichmann was sent to Hungary to wipe out the Jews. He sent nearly four hundred thousand Hungarian Jews to their deaths between May 15 and July 1, 1944.[18]

Eichmann relished his reputation as one of Hitler's most successful persecutors of Jews. When he called the Jewish Council to meet at his headquarters in Budapest, he said, "You know who I am, don't you? I am the one known as the bloodhound."[19] Wallenberg's arrival on July 9 began a frustrating series of setbacks to Eichmann's plans. Wallenberg played a key role in preventing Eichmann from sending all the Jews in Hungary to their deaths.

Eichmann was captured at the end of the war, but escaped to Argentina. He lived there until Israeli agents found him in 1960. In Israel, he was tried for crimes against the Jewish people. He was hanged there on May 31, 1962.[20]

territory. The WRB tried to persuade the International Committee of the Red Cross (ICRC) to help, but leading rescue operations to free political prisoners was not part of the ICRC's mission. According to historian Randolph Braham, "The I[C]RC believed that intervention on behalf of the civilian persecutees—the Jews—not only was beyond its scope but would actually jeopardize its traditional activities in support of prisoners of war."[21] Instead, it promised to send the WRB updates on treatment of the Jews as reported by the Hungarian Red Cross and made arrangements to provide Jewish prisoners with food and clothing. The WRB asked both Protestant and Catholic leaders of the world to help rescue Jews. President Roosevelt even appealed to Hungarian Gentiles, asking that they help their Jewish countrymen. He threatened that those who aided the Germans in the destruction of the Jews would later be tried as war criminals.

The Truth About Auschwitz

On April 7, 1944, two Jews escaped from the Auschwitz concentration camp in Poland. They traveled to Zilina, Slovakia, where they contacted the Jewish Council and made a full report of all they had observed in Auschwitz.[22] The report later became known as the "Auschwitz Protocols." Rudolf Vrba and Alfred Wetzler told of the thousands of innocent people who arrived on trains at Auschwitz day after day. Those who appeared strong enough to do physical labor were led away. The other prisoners, dehydrated, hungry, and filthy from riding for days in the cattle cars, were told they must line up to go into the shower building. Once they were locked inside, the Zyklon B canisters were released. Meanwhile, Jewish workers, under the watchful eye of the SS officers, searched any luggage the prisoners had brought and confiscated any valuables they found. Vrba and Wetzler drew

23

maps of the camp for the Jewish council, showing the locations of gas chambers and crematoria.

One frightening part of their story concerned a major construction project at the camp. Vrba observed Jewish workers beginning a large project near the railroad ramps. One worker, a friend of Vrba's, told him the reason for the project: "He had overheard from the SS that a million Hungarian Jews would be arriving soon, and that the unloading system on the old ramp would be unable to handle such masses of people with sufficient speed."[23]

Trains began rolling from the Hungarian provinces on May 15. They carried as many as ten thousand to twelve thousand people a day to Auschwitz. The Nazis maintained that these people were being taken to labor camps to aid the German war effort. Some prisoners were selected by the guards and forced to write postcards that would appear to come from a summer resort in Austria called Waldsee. The postcards carried messages such as, "All well. I am working here."[24] Waldsee did not exist. The cards, delivered to families of those deported, were intended to calm those Jews left behind. Some of the cards, however, carried the secret they were meant to hide: a message written in Hebrew that told the real fate of those sent to "Waldsee."[25]

In the city of Budapest, the lives of the Jews had also changed dramatically. Like in other areas of Europe, Jews were required to wear a yellow star on their clothing. Any Jew caught without the star could be immediately executed. They were ordered to stay in their homes except for specific hours of the day, and they were only allowed to buy limited amounts of food and supplies. The Germans froze the bank accounts of wealthy Jews and, through the Jewish Council, demanded the Jews supply them with household

Adolf Eichmann played a key role in the deportations of hundreds of thousands of Hungarian Jews. During his trial in Israel, he sat in a bullet-proof box. The Israelis feared that Eichmann might be assassinated before justice could be served.

goods such as silverware, glasses, rugs, and even fine paintings and pianos for the use of the German officers. Eichmann assured the Jews that if they followed orders they would not be harmed. Many in the capital still held hope that they would survive until either the Allies or the Soviets could liberate them. However, unbeknownst to them, the Auschwitz Protocols suggested that the extermination of Hungarian Jews would proceed at the fastest pace the Nazis could arrange.

Something must be done immediately. It would take a hero.

A Chance to
Save Lives

By June 1944, little progress had been made toward slowing Eichmann's deportation of Hungarian Jews to death camps. Jewish leaders suggested that the Allies bomb the railroad tracks to Auschwitz and the crematoria there. The United States War Department and the British decided against it, however, stating that they did not want to take bombers away from the war front, nor risk lives of Allied airmen for a nonmilitary mission.[1]

"Blood for Trucks"

One attempt to negotiate with the Nazis for Jewish lives ended in disappointment. Joel Brand of the Rescue and Relief Committee of Budapest attempted to obtain the release of concentration camp prisoners. The Nazis offered to give up one million Jews to the Allies in exchange for ten thousand trucks needed for Germany's war effort.[2]

The deal was uncertain from the beginning. The Allies did not trust the Nazis and feared they would not release the prisoners as promised. Eichmann also insisted that the Jews released could not return to Hungary, as his mission for Hitler's Nazi regime was to make Hungary *judenrein*, or free of Jews. Although many Jewish Hungarians would want to go to Palestine, Eichmann had promised the Arab leader of Palestine that he would not allow any more Jews to go there. Allied countries were reluctant to accept too many Jewish immigrants. The Soviets objected to the deal, because the other Allies wanted assurance that the promised trucks would only be used on the eastern war front, the side where the Germans were fighting the Soviets. Brand went to the Middle East to participate in the negotiations, but he was arrested by the British on June 5 and imprisoned in Cairo as a spy for the Germans. The deal was never made. Years later, Brand believed that the offer was a hoax arranged by Heinrich Himmler to distract the Allies from other negotiations between Germany and the western allies against the Soviets.[3]

On June 6, the Allies landed at Normandy. It appeared that the Germans would soon be defeated, but that threat only made Eichmann's job of killing the Jews more urgent. If he truly wanted to rid Hungary of the Jews, he would have to finish the job quickly, before the Allies could implement a plan to rescue them.

Wanted: Foreign Observers

The War Refugee Board (WRB) was working on just such a plan. Because the WRB was an American organization, it could not send representatives into enemy-controlled territory. Several countries had chosen to remain neutral in World War II. The WRB wanted to work through the neutral countries that already had embassies (called legations) in Hungary. A message from Cordell Hull, United States secretary of state, to Herschel V. Johnson, United States minister to Sweden, urged Johnson to convince the neutral Swedish government to send more diplomats into Hungary as "foreign observers" to "persuade individuals and officials to desist from further barbarisms."[4] Later, the WRB representative in Stockholm, Iver Olsen, reported that the WRB would pledge up to one hundred thousand dollars to help begin a program to rescue Hungarian Jews. The American Jewish Joint Distribution Committee (JDC), an American organization funded by private citizens for aid to persecuted Jews overseas, would match the WRB pledge.[5]

On June 12, Olsen met with a group of prominent Swedish Jews to discuss the proposition. Among those present was Koloman Lauer, Wallenberg's employer. Olsen asked the committee to find a suitable Swedish Gentile to go into Budapest to lead the rescue effort. Lauer suggested Wallenberg, but others on the committee felt he was too young and inexperienced for the job. Wallenberg met with Olsen and with Swedish chief rabbi, Dr. Marcus Ehrenpreis. Both were impressed with Wallenberg and gave their approval. Later, Wallenberg met with Herschel Johnson, who also approved him.

Wallenberg's Demands

When Wallenberg finally met with the Swedish Foreign Office to receive appointment as an official diplomat, he knew enough about diplomatic policy and about German bureaucracy to understand the obstacles he might face. He was not willing to accept the job if he was destined to fail from the beginning, so he presented a list of demands before agreeing to accept the job. He wanted to be able to negotiate with Hungarian and German leaders, and he wanted to be able to offer protection for Jews inside Swedish buildings. He wanted to be sure he had enough money to provide aid and even to use bribery if necessary. Wallenberg was requesting privileges far beyond those usually allowed diplomats, especially newly-appointed personnel. The Swedish Foreign Office considered Wallenberg's demands for over a week before granting its approval on June 23.

Wallenberg planned to travel to Budapest to begin his new position on August 1. When he studied the current situation in Hungary, however, he decided to go sooner. Eichmann's deportation program had already transported over 437,000 Jews from the Hungarian countryside.[6] Virtually no Jews remained except for those in Budapest. Wallenberg told Lauer, "I cannot stay in Sweden beyond the beginning of July. Every day costs human lives."[7]

Hard Times in Budapest

In June 1944, new laws further restricting the freedom of Jewish citizens had just become effective in Budapest. They were forced to move from their homes to apartments in the Pest district, east of the Danube River. These buildings were marked with the Jewish star to identify them. The Jews could only leave their apartments between 2:00 P.M. and 5:00 P.M. Jewish doctors were only allowed to treat Jewish patients. Within the city, two hundred thirty thousand Jews lived in fear that any day the Germans would come to take them away.[8]

The Hungarian government had changed dramatically since the German occupation. When Hitler forced Kállay to resign, he replaced him with General Döme Sztójay, a loyal pro-Nazi. He decided to keep Miklós Horthy as Hungarian regent, because he believed Horthy would be intimidated into remaining loyal to the Reich. Horthy cooperated with Eichmann's deportation program of the Hungarian Jews from the provinces, but he still wanted to have the power to make

29

decisions for Hungary without the influence of the Germans. Between June 25 and June 30, Horthy received letters from the Roman Catholic Pope, President Roosevelt, and King Gustav V of Sweden. All asked him to act quickly to save the Jews. Gustav's message included this plea: "I permit myself to turn to your highness personally, to beg in the name of humanity that you take measures to save those who still remain to be saved of this unfortunate people."[9] Both the United States and Great Britain warned him that after the war he could be charged for war crimes against the Jews. On July 7, he bowed to this international pressure and canceled the deportations of Hungarian citizens to the death camps.

"In a Hurry to Get to Work"

On Wallenberg's last night in Stockholm, he invited a few friends to his apartment for a farewell dinner. He told them, "I am going to leave you now for one reason: to save as many lives as possible; to rescue Jews from the claws of those murderers."[10] On July 6, he left for Budapest, stopping first in Berlin, Germany, to visit his sister, Nina, who was married to a Swedish diplomat stationed there. When Nina informed him that his travel arrangements to Budapest had been made for July 9, he declared that there was no time to waste and he must leave on the next train.[11] Thus, he found himself aboard a train from Berlin to Budapest on July 8. The train was already fully booked with German soldiers, so Wallenberg had no seat. He spent the entire trip sitting on his backpack.

Per Anger was already at work in the Swedish legation in Budapest. He met Wallenberg at the train station. "He was carrying two knapsacks, a sleeping bag, a windbreaker, and a revolver," said Anger. "'The revolver is just to give me courage,' he said to me in his typically joking way. 'I hope I never have to use it. But now I'm in a hurry to get to work.'"[12]

International Efforts to Help the Jews

Although the situation still looked very dangerous for the Budapest Jews, there were some rescue missions already operating in the summer of 1944. A few weeks before Wallenberg arrived, Horthy had considered a Swiss plan for about seven thousand Hungarian Jews to emigrate to Palestine. Although the planned emigration did not happen, it did show Horthy's willingness to consider the possibility of allowing Jewish people to leave Hungary for other countries rather than being transported to death camps by the Nazis. In June, a diplomat was sent by the El Salvadoran government with citizenship papers. The Spanish produced papers to allow five hundred children to emigrate to Tangier. Swiss diplomat Carl Lutz began issuing "aliyah certificates," documents allowing Jews to emigrate to British-controlled Palestine, and the government of Switzerland agreed to accept between five thousand and ten thousand children as refugees.[13] The International Red Cross, although it was unwilling to take on the job of transporting people out of the country, did ask to be allowed to help provide food and clothing for Jewish people. The Swedish legation was ready to expand its rescue efforts as well, and Wallenberg was ready to help.

The Schutz-Pass

At the time Wallenberg arrived, some of the pressure had been relieved, since Horthy had stopped the deportations of Jews. Still, this seemed like a temporary situation, and the deportations could resume at any moment. Upon his arrival in Budapest, Wallenberg immediately sat down with Anger to discuss the steps the Swedish legation was already taking to help the Jewish people of Budapest. Anger and his staff had been issuing some passports based on applications for

31

Swedish citizenship. A passport indicated that the person named on it would be emigrating to Sweden. These Jews could not travel immediately, because they would have to cross through Germany or other Nazi-controlled countries in order to reach Sweden. They would be expected to leave Hungary as soon as travel was possible after the war. Strictly speaking, Anger could only issue such provisional passports to Swedish citizens and those with family or business interests in Sweden. Because those people who had these documents were considered to be Swedish citizens, they did not have to wear the yellow star like other Hungarian Jews.

Soon, Anger and his staff had issued over seven hundred of these passes, and more people appeared at the legation every day requesting passes.[14] Wallenberg wanted to make more of them and make them better, so he created a new pass. It included the three crowns of Sweden and was printed in blue and yellow. The new passes looked more professional than the ones Anger's staff had been using. The Hungarian Foreign Ministry gave him permission to issue fifteen hundred of the new Schutz-passes. Later, Wallenberg convinced them to allow him to give out forty-five hundred.[15]

Eichmann's Deception

Since July 7, Eichmann had been frustrated by Horthy's order to halt the deportations. Eichmann complained to his superiors, but they supported Horthy's order. Eichmann,

This Schutz-pass was issued by the Swedish legation in Budapest to Hungarian Jew Lili Katz. Documents like this saved thousands of lives.

SCHUTZ-PASS

Nr. 28/69.

Name: **L i l i   K a t z**
Név:

Wohnort: **Budapest**
Lakás:

Geburtsdatum: **13.Sept.1913.**
Születési ideje:

Geburtsort: **Budapest**
Születési helye:

Körperlänge: **164 cm.**
Magasság:

Haarfarbe: **blond** **Augenfarbe:** **grau**
Hajszín: *Szemszín:*

Unterschrift:
Aláírás:

SCHWEDEN

SVÉDORSZÁG

Die Kgl. Schwedische Gesandtschaft in Budapest bestätigt, dass der Obengenannte im Rahmen der — von dem Kgl. Schwedischen Aussenministerium autorisierten — Repatriierung nach Schweden reisen wird. Der Betreffende ist auch in einen Kollektivpass eingetragen.

Bis Abreise steht der Obengenannte und seine Wohnung unter dem Schutz der Kgl. Schwedischen Gesandtschaft in Budapest.

Gültigkeit: erlischt 14 Tage nach Einreise nach Schweden.

A budapesti Svéd Kir. Követség igazolja, hogy fentnevezett — a Svéd Kir. Külügyminisztérium által jóváhagyott — repatriálás keretében Svédországba utazik.

Nevezett a kollektiv útlevélben is szerepel.

Elutazásáig fentnevezett és lakása a budapesti Svéd Kir. Követség oltalma alatt áll.

Érvényét veszti a Svédországba való megérkezéstől számított tizennegyedik napon.

Reiseberechtigung nur gemeinsam mit dem Kollektivpass. Einreisewisum wird nur in dem Kollektivpass eingetragen.

Budapest, den **25.August** 1944

KÖNIGLICH SCHWEDISCHE GESANDTSCHAFT
SVÉD KIRÁLYI KÖVETSÉG

Kgl. Schwedischer Gesandte

Antiqua Nyomdai és Irodalmi Rt. Budapest
9387 F. Wenner Emil

Per Anger

Born December 7, 1913, in Gothenberg, Sweden, Per Johan Valentin Anger began his first diplomatic job at the Swedish legation office in Berlin, Germany in 1940. In 1942, he was assigned to the Swedish legation in Budapest. After the invasion of Hungary, Anger and his staff issued Swedish passports to Hungarian Jews, but could only give out seven hundred. Wallenberg's influence allowed the department to help many more. Anger accompanied Wallenberg to train stations to rescue Jewish prisoners and to distribute food.

On January 10, 1945, Anger urged Wallenberg to interrupt his rescue efforts and move to the Buda side of the city, as both Eichmann and the Arrow Cross had threatened to kill him. Wallenberg refused, saying, "I'd never be able to go back to Stockholm without knowing that I'd done all a man could do to save as many Jews as possible."[16]

After the war, Anger continued to serve as a Swedish diplomat in many countries. In 1982, he was named "Righteous Among the Nations" by the organization for Holocaust Remembrance, Yad Vashem. For years, Anger led efforts to try to gain Wallenberg's release from the Russians. Anger called Wallenberg, "one of the greatest humanitarians in modern times."[17]

Per Anger died of natural causes in Stockholm, Sweden, August 25, 2002.

however, was not ready to accept defeat. He intended to continue the deportations, in defiance of Horthy's order. Fifteen hundred Jewish prisoners were detained in a camp called Kistarcsa, just outside Budapest. The group included lawyers, journalists, and other prominent Jews from Budapest. On July 12, Eichmann ordered his officers to load the prisoners onto a train and send them to Auschwitz. A Hungarian guard at the camp, however, managed to alert the Jewish Council. The council made contact with the neutral legations and several religious leaders, who immediately sent protests to Horthy. Horthy had the train stopped before it could reach the Hungarian border. The prisoners were returned to the camp.[18]

A few days later, Eichmann tried a different approach. On July 19, he called a meeting at 8:00 A.M. of the Jewish Council at his headquarters at the Hotel Majestic. He held them for nearly twelve hours at the hotel, refusing to let them leave or use the telephones. By the time he released them at 7:30 P.M., over twelve hundred of the Kistarcsa prisoners had been deported and were already outside Hungary.[19]

Opening Section C

Wallenberg immediately began establishing his operation and finding workers to assist him. He called his new division at the legation Section C. His workers were volunteers, Jews who needed protection. Wallenberg's staff members were not required to wear the yellow star. This allowed them to travel about Budapest with more freedom. They also could remain living in their own homes, instead of moving into the yellow-star houses. Wallenberg needed many people to help produce the Schutz-passes. Every day, hundreds of people lined up in the street outside Wallenberg's office seeking passes. With the curfew allowing Jews to be out of their homes only two hours a day, many went home disappointed every day.

Wallenberg did his best to be fair with the distribution of the passes, and also to help as many people as possible. He gave one pass per family, with the hope that the Nazis would not deport family members of a "Swedish citizen." He numbered the passes, but did not number them in order, so that counterfeit passes would not be as easy to spot. He gave out passes in the order of the people lined up each day in front of the legation, and he did not allow his staff to move friends or relatives to the front of the line. He even fired two staff members whom he thought had accepted bribes to move certain applications to the top of the pile.[20] He knew forty-five hundred passes would not be enough, but perhaps he could slow Hitler's plan to exterminate the Budapest Jews.

Assassination Attempt on Hitler

But Hitler had bigger problems than Wallenberg's rescue effort. On July 20, Major Claus von Stauffenberg walked into a meeting with Hitler, carrying a briefcase containing a bomb. He set the case down and left the room. The bomb exploded, killing four people and leaving Hitler injured, but very much alive. The assassination attempt had been planned for years, with its planners waiting for just the right opportunity. For the next few weeks, the German leadership was in an uproar with accusations and executions of top Nazi officers. In Hungary, Eichmann waited for Hitler to overrule Horthy's order to stop deporting Jews, but Hitler was more concerned with events in Berlin than Budapest.

Wallenberg's workload was overwhelming at times, but so was his mission. Every day brought the Jews closer to total annihilation. Wallenberg's office was still limited to producing only forty-five hundred passes, and the deportations could begin again any day. In his first letter home, Wallenberg told his mother, "We are incredibly busy and have been working day and night." In the same letter, he asked his mother to break the sad news to Koloman Lauer and his wife that Mrs. Lauer's parents and a young child of the family had been sent to a concentration camp and were probably dead.[21]

Wallenberg was determined to find another way to help the Jews.

4

Hope for the Jews

By early August, Wallenberg was working harder than ever. He posted signs all over Budapest to announce the validity of the Schutz-passes and be sure that all Hungarian police and German SS officers knew what they looked like.[1] He was able to expand the legation into the two buildings on either side of the original building. He brought in medical personnel to staff a small hospital there. Food was rationed in Budapest, and rationed even more strictly for Jewish households than for Gentiles. Wallenberg's newly expanded legation included a soup kitchen to feed the poor.

He set up printing presses in the basement of the legation and increased his staff. Despite the exhausting work, Wallenberg seemed fully absorbed in his mission. In a letter to his mother on August 6, Wallenberg described his time in Budapest as, "the 3–4 most interesting weeks of my life, even though we are surrounded by a tragedy of immeasurable proportions."[2]

Swedish Houses and the International Ghetto

His next move would be a bit more complicated. He feared that the star-marked Jewish houses would make it too easy for Eichmann's officers to round up their victims whenever the deportations would resume. He had already gained permission to offer safety within the Swedish legation buildings, but they could not hold many people. He needed to expand, but in order to do that, he would need the permission of the Hungarian government. He would have to deal with the head of the Hungarian gendarmes, Colonel Laszlo Ferenczy. Ferenczy had played a leading role in Eichmann's deportation of the Jews from the countryside of Hungary. Without the manpower of the Hungarian officers, the Germans could not have deported nearly half a million Jews in only six weeks. Ferenczy would not favor any plan to help save the Jewish citizens of Budapest.

Wallenberg arranged a meeting with Colonel Ferenczy. Since Wallenberg did not speak Hungarian, he took Elizabeth Kasser, a Red Cross volunteer, as an interpreter. According to Kasser, "Ferenczy came to us and made a long speech about how we should be ashamed of ourselves for helping Jews, and what awful people Jews are."[3] In spite of his angry words, Ferenczy gave permission for Wallenberg to rent three houses for six hundred fifty Jews. He also allowed the Red Cross to set up some houses as well. When Wallenberg returned to his office, he had his staff hang large Swedish flags next to the Jewish stars on the new Swedish buildings.[4]

International Help

Other neutral countries and relief agencies were also working to help the Jews of Budapest. Swiss diplomat Carl Lutz coordinated a large rescue operation from the Swiss legation building on Vadasz Street in Budapest. It was called the Glass

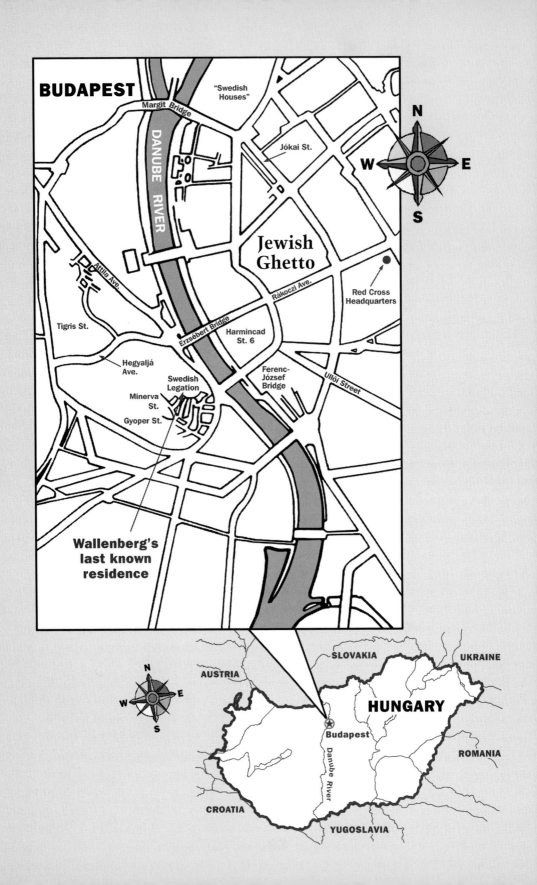

House because it was donated to the Swiss by a manufacturer of glass and ceramics. It housed Lutz's printing presses where Swiss protective passes were manufactured. Lutz had been printing his passes before Wallenberg arrived in Budapest, but they were not as "official-looking" as Wallenberg's passes, since they did not carry any official seals or identification photos. Still, they were effective.

As Lutz and Wallenberg's methods proved successful, other nations joined them. Other countries set up their own houses for those who held their passes, creating what became known as an international ghetto of Hungarian Jews claiming citizenship of nearly every country except Hungary. The ghetto expanded during the next few months as Wallenberg and the other diplomats added more houses.

The International Red Cross also increased its efforts to help. It set up houses for Jewish children. The head of this effort, known as Section A, was Ottó Komoly of the Zionist Rescue and Relief Committee. Komoly recruited members of a Zionist youth organization to help with the children. The first house opened in August; later others were added. Nearly six thousand children were aided by the Section A operation.[5]

The Red Cross also sought the help of religious organizations. Some Jews went to Protestant churches to be baptized, but the Nazis refused to honor the papers of any Jews who had converted to other religions after the German invasion of

Budapest was where Raoul Wallenberg did most of his work. He divided his time between the Swedish Legation, his Üllöi Street Headquarters, and his Budapest residence. He succeeded in getting many Jewish people moved from the ghetto to Swedish safe houses hear the Danube River.

March 1944. The Red Cross formed a new department, Section B, to help those converts who were still considered Jewish by the government. Religious institutions like monasteries managed to help hide two thousand children.[6]

Too Many Passes?

By the middle of August, more than twenty thousand people had applied for Schutz-passes, but Wallenberg only had permission to distribute forty-five hundred of them. Those who had passes worried that the great number of the papers being issued would make the Nazis stop honoring them. Even the Swedish government seemed worried about Wallenberg's work. In a letter to the War Refugee Board, Iver Olsen reported:

> . . . the Swedish foreign office is somewhat uneasy about Wallenberg's activities in Budapest and perhaps feel that he has jumped in with too big a splash. They would prefer, of course, to approach the Jewish problem in the finest traditions of European diplomacy, which wouldn't help too much.[7]

Since well over two hundred thousand Jews lived in Budapest, and Wallenberg, Lutz, the Red Cross, and other agencies were limited in the number of passes they could give, it is not surprising that counterfeit passes soon appeared. A Polish Jew named Boris Teicholz ran one counterfeiting operation. Teicholz was printing Schutz-passes, as well as other documents such as false certificates of baptism. The latter were meant to convince the Nazis that the person holding the certificate was a Catholic or Lutheran. Wallenberg knew about Teicholz's operation, but did not interfere, since he knew he could only legally produce forty-five hundred passes. If Teicholz could help save more people, then

Carl Lutz was born in Switzerland in 1895. He went to school in the United States, then entered diplomatic service as the Swiss Consul in Palestine in 1935. During World War II, he helped German citizens who were to be deported from Palestine as enemy aliens.

In 1942, Lutz was sent to Budapest. The work he had done in Palestine to help German citizens gained him the permission of the Germans to issue seven thousand passports for Jews to emigrate to Palestine.[8] When the Arrow Cross began the labor draft, Lutz and Wallenberg went together every day to Teleki Square, where the Arrow Cross gathered Jewish men to be sent to labor camps. The two diplomats rescued thousands of people.[9]

Lutz did not have the blessing of his government to rescue Jews; he acted on his own. He escaped the Russians and returned to his own country after the war. Instead of praising his work in Budapest, the Swiss government reprimanded Lutz for issuing passports without Swiss permission.[10]

Despite the attitude of his government, Lutz did not regret his conduct. Many years later he said, "In Budapest I knew no fear. The humanist in me held sway. I acted in accordance with my convictions."[11] In 1965, Lutz was named "Righteous Among the Nations" by Yad Vashem. In 1975, he died in Switzerland.

Carl Lutz helped Jews emigrate to Palestine. Ruth Kohn and her daughter Rena took a ship to Palestine in 1938.

Wallenberg would go along with it, and encourage Lutz and other diplomats to do the same.[12]

Resuming Deportations

Despite Wallenberg's efforts and the establishment of the international ghetto, the danger to the Budapest Jews was still very real. On August 17, 1944, Eichmann sent the German Gestapo to capture Dr. Samu Stern and two other members

Adolf Eichmann did whatever he could to deport Jews to death camps.

of the Jewish Council. The men were interrogated and beaten by the Gestapo. One of the council members, László Petö, had a letter from Wallenberg with him. According to Petö, "The Gestapo investigator, who seemed a bit drunk, was obviously incensed by the Wallenberg letter and mistreated me severely."[13] Horthy learned of this action and ordered the council members released. They were returned within twenty-four hours.

On August 18, the Germans arranged a parade of SS soldiers through downtown Budapest. Nazi soldiers marched through the city, accompanied by tanks and armored personnel carriers. Eichmann was planning to begin deportations again. Over the next few days, however, the situation changed. The series of events confused and frustrated almost everyone, but no one more than Eichmann. Wallenberg and members of the other neutral legations learned about the deportation plan. On August 21, they sent a protest to Horthy. "The Envoys of the neutral States represented in Budapest have been acquainted with the fact that the deportation of the Jews is about to be accomplished. They all know what this means, even though it be described as 'labour service.'"[14] They demanded that Horthy stop it.

Horthy Stands Up to Eichmann

On August 23, 1944, Romania—Hungary's neighboring country to the southeast—surrendered to the Soviet Union and declared war on both Germany and Hungary. Horthy was now certain that Germany would soon lose the war, and he was aware of the Allies' threats to punish those who cooperated with the Nazis' plan for Jewish annihilation. He decided it would be wise to stop the deportation. Ferenczy was also convinced that Hungary could be destroyed by Germany's enemies. He reversed his previous support of the Germans.

45

He pledged to back Horthy's decision with the force of the Hungarian gendarmes against Eichmann's men, if necessary.

Eichmann was furious when Ferenczy told him they would not cooperate with the deportations. He threatened to arrest and torture Ferenczy, then sent a telegram to Berlin. He hoped that Hitler would order the deportations to proceed. On August 24, Hitler's SS leader, Heinrich Himmler, replied that the war effort was more important than the deportations, and the plan was canceled.[15] Eichmann felt that he could do nothing more. He left Hungary.

New Hungarian Leadership

On August 25, Allied troops entered Paris and liberated it. German defeat seemed certain. Horthy was convinced he must get rid of the pro-Nazi Hungarian government so that the new government could "save whatever can be saved."[16] He fired pro-Nazi Prime Minister Sztójay whom Hitler had appointed. He replaced him with General Géza Lakatos, the head of the Hungarian army. Like Horthy, Lakatos believed this was their last chance to save Hungary from the Germans.[17]

Horthy knew the Germans would not like this show of independence, but he still wanted to find a way out of the war before Germany went down in defeat, taking Hungary with her. Meanwhile, Wallenberg and the Jews of Budapest took refuge in their protected houses while Allied bombs hit the city. They felt safer for the moment.

5

Power Struggle

The end of August may have held disappointment for Eichmann, but it brought unexpected, although temporary, relief for Wallenberg, Lutz, and others who hoped to protect the remaining Jews of Budapest. The growing international ghetto, Eichmann's departure, the new Hungarian government under Géza Lakatos, and the increasing number of organizations working to help the Jews gave them reason for hope. Regent Horthy tried to convince the Nazi leadership that he was still loyal to the Reich, but he refused to allow the deportations to begin again.[1]

Wallenberg continued his rescue work by issuing more Schutz-passes. He also increased the number of buildings in the international ghetto and requested the government to release Jewish laborers who were being held in camps within Hungary. The Soviet army was advancing from Romania deeper into Hungary each day. Most Hungarians believed that the Germans would soon be defeated and the war would be over. When the Allies took over Hungary, there would be no need for further rescue efforts.

Wallenberg's letter to his mother that September spoke of frequent air raids, "forcing us to sit in the air-raid shelter for three or four hours on end."[2] In his letter to Stockholm on September 12, he reported that he had staff working both day and night shifts to process applications for protective passes, but he was expecting the workload to slow down soon, and he hoped to be able to begin reducing staff and phasing out some parts of Section C by September 17. Still, he was concerned that the German retreat from Hungary might include last minute attacks against the Jews in an effort to destroy them before they could be freed by the Allies.[3]

Horthy Versus the Germans

Horthy's new government did not please the Germans. They believed the new prime minister, Géza Lakatos, was too friendly to the Allies and not willing to fully support the German army in the war.[4] Horthy had ignored most of Veesenmayer's suggestions for cabinet members for the new Hungarian government. Instead, he had chosen men loyal to him and to Hungarian independence from Germany. Horthy chose only three pro-Nazi members to be in his cabinet. Miklós Bonczos was appointed minister of the interior and Lajos Reményi-Schneller was named finance minister. Vessenmayer's choice for deputy prime minister, Béla Jurcsek, was made agriculture and supply minister. Although the three were part of the cabinet, their relatively minor positions left them without much decision-making power.[5]

The people of Hungary were also divided in their loyalties. Some were strong supporters of Horthy and Lakatos. Others, thinking that the Soviets would soon be in control, were forming communist groups. Some Hungarians still remained loyal to the Germans. Ferenc Szálasi, a Hungarian pro-German fanatic, was leader of the Hungarian Nazi party, the Nyilas party. He had built up his own militaristic unit, the Arrow Cross. Szálasi recruited thousands of members, many of them illiterate teenage boys from the slums of Budapest. He gave each one a green uniform, a loaded rifle, and an armband with the symbol of crossed red arrows. The new recruits were fed anti-Semitic propaganda that dehumanized the Jews. They were taught that killing a Jew was no more significant than swatting a fly. They were also taught that their first allegiance was to the German Reich, not to Lakatos' government.

The new Hungarian government wanted to keep control over Hungary's affairs instead of bowing to German pressure. It also wanted to give some protection to the Hungarian Jews while Horthy tried to make peace with the Allies. The Germans were not pleased with Horthy's refusal to send Jews out of Hungary to the death camps. They reluctantly agreed to stop the deportations, but only if Horthy would allow the Jews of Budapest to be sent to labor camps in the Hungarian countryside.

Wallenberg and the other neutral diplomats objected to these camps, because they feared that the Jews held there would become easy targets for deportation. The Arrow Cross could quickly load the prisoners from the camps onto trains bound for death camps. The neutrals also worried that the near-defeated Nazi army might destroy the Jews to prevent their rescue by Allies. German bombers could target the camps. Troops driven back from the battlefields in Hungary by the Soviets might take out their frustrations by slaughtering labor camp prisoners.

Although Horthy agreed to the labor camp plan, he insisted that the camps must be inspected by the International Red

Cross and must meet its standards of acceptable conditions for health and humane treatment. For several weeks, the Red Cross inspected different sites in the Hungarian countryside as possible locations for camps, but they did not find any that met acceptable standards. On September 29, Wallenberg reported to the Swedish embassy: "The agreement between the Hungarians and the Germans that Budapest was to be emptied of its Jewish population . . . has hitherto been totally sabotaged by the Hungarian authorities. Not a single Jew has left the capital."[6]

Help for Jewish Workers

Wallenberg also began a new campaign to save Jews. Over fifty thousand Jewish men were working in labor battalions attached to Hungarian army units. Warm clothing and food were distributed to the soldiers first, so many of the Jewish workers were poorly fed and wore only summer clothing. Wallenberg worried that the coming cold weather would bring sickness and death to many of them. He persuaded Lakatos to separate those Jews who held protective passes from the army battalions and return them to work in Budapest. They were reassigned to the city to clear debris from the bombings. Wallenberg housed them in Swedish buildings and in reopened Jewish synagogues.

One worker, László Ernster, had been forced to leave medical school when he was drafted into a work battalion in 1943. During his absence, his wife applied for and received a Swedish pass. Although he had not been allowed any contact with his family, he learned of the pass one day when his work battalion boarded a streetcar on which his wife was already a passenger. When Lakatos allowed the reassignment of protected Jews, Ernster was released from the work camp to return to Budapest. Each day he reported to the synagogue, and each night he was able to return home to his family. Ernster and his forty fellow workers in the Swedish Company did not have to wear the yellow star, although they did wear a yellow armband during their work hours. According to Ernster, "We all quickly forgot our past sufferings and for the first time in months we felt like human beings again."[7]

By the middle of September, fewer than four hundred fifty Jewish laborers were being detained in camps in Hungary, and some Jews in Budapest even dared to remove the yellow stars from their clothing.[8] Although they had been limited to only two hours a day outside their homes just two months before, now many began ignoring the curfews.

Horthy's Dilemma

Regent Horthy wanted to get out of the war. Although he wanted Hungary to be free of German rule, he did not want the communist Soviets to take over the country. Lakatos, as prime minister, had a difficult job. He had to convince the Germans that the Hungarian government was still loyal, stall on the matter of resuming deportations, and provide cover for Horthy's efforts to withdraw from the war. Horthy's first tactic was to demand that Germany send additional troops to help defend Hungary. If Hitler refused, then it would give Horthy the chance to withdraw with honor. Horthy indicated that his troops were near defeat in southern Hungary. If German forces did not arrive to help, the Hungarians would be forced to surrender to the Soviets. The Germans agreed to send help, but they also warned that they would not tolerate any Hungarian move to desert the German cause. They were clearly suspicious.

Next, Horthy tried to negotiate with the western Allies in order to avoid Soviet invasion. Through former British Ambassador George Bakách-Bessenyey, Horthy sent a

message indicating Hungary's intention to surrender to the Allies, but he asked for several considerations. First, he asked the Allies to help defend his borders from the Soviets and Romanians. Next, he specified that Allied troops only be allowed to occupy areas necessary for battle strategy. To lessen the destruction of the country, he also asked that the Allies let German troops leave Hungary without further battles.[9] The Allies rejected his offer. Horthy's only way out of the war was to surrender to the Soviets.

More Passes and Aid Needed

German soldiers were everywhere. In a rare show of armed resistance, Jewish rebels planted a bomb in a German army barracks on September 29.[10] In revenge, German soldiers invaded several of the yellow-star houses in the Jewish ghetto. They beat the inhabitants and took some to detention camps. Each day more people came to Wallenberg's office seeking protective passes. He reported that his office had around eight thousand applications that had not yet been processed. Although he had begun decreasing his staff just two weeks before, he now added people in order to handle the massive amount of paperwork.[11]

Wallenberg continued to work to ease the suffering of the Jews. Conditions in both the Jewish (yellow-star) houses and the international ghetto (the protected houses) were not

Per Anger was second secretary at the Swedish legation in Budapest during World War II and worked with Raoul Wallenberg in efforts to rescue Hungarian Jews. Anger is pictured in his office. A portrait of Wallenberg is in the background.

pleasant. Most Jewish houses were overcrowded. In the international ghetto, more than fifteen thousand people were living in buildings that before the war had housed fewer than four thousand people.[12] Since most Jews were forbidden to work, they had little or no money for food. Even with money, rations were so limited that they could not buy enough to feed everyone.

In mid-September, Wallenberg received a check for $100,000 from Iver Olsen of the War Refugee Board. In his report on September 29, he describes his distribution of the money. About two-thirds was given to the Jewish Council for food for the soup kitchen and for clothing. Some of the money was given to an orphanage that had been bombed. Some was given in cash to the needy. Some money was spent for food to be stored in case the coming Soviet invasion caused a food shortage.[13]

At the beginning of October, the Jewish Council discovered that some Hungarian Jews deported to Austria were still alive in camps there. They asked Wallenberg if he could send aid to them. He made arrangements with the Swedish Red Cross to send medicine and clothing to the prisoners. By October 15, they had sent out thirty thousand packages of clothing.[14] He also worked with the El Salvadoran consulate to grant Salvadoran citizenship to Jews, some of whom had already gained Swedish protection.

Many of the Jewish workers in labor camps were not so fortunate. On October 11, Jewish Labor Service Company number 101/322 arrived at the Kiskunhalas train station. At the station, they were met by another company of Jewish workers. The men of 101/322 shared their food rations with the second company. This act of kindness was punished by the SS and Arrow Cross guards. They killed 194 members of Company 101/322.[15]

Shaky Allegiance

The war was going badly for the Germans. They were defeated in a tank battle with the Soviets near the city of Debrecen, 120 miles east of Budapest. Soviet troops continued to advance toward Budapest. During this period, Prime Minister Lakatos held daily meetings with Foreign Minister Gusztáv Hennyey and Defense Minister Lajos Csatay to discuss their strategies. No mention of their plans could be made in cabinet meetings where the three pro-Nazi cabinet members were Veesenmayer's ears. It was not easy to keep their discussions secret. The Germans had agents everywhere who kept a close watch on messengers who came in and out of the palace. Soon, nearly everyone in Budapest, including Wallenberg, knew that Horthy was trying to make a deal with the Soviets.[16]

Changing sides in the middle of the war was risky. The Hungarian soldiers on the battlefield were currently fighting on the German side against the Soviets and Romanians. Surrendering to the Soviets would mean that the Hungarian soldiers would suddenly stop resisting the Soviets and would instead declare war on the Germans. How could Horthy communicate this change of allegiance to the troops? Would the soldiers be willing to suddenly switch sides, would they resist, or just desert the battlefield in confusion? Horthy believed that most of his top military leaders were loyal to him. He did not know how many of the mid-level commanders would support him and how many would instead support a German effort to rise up and take over the Hungarian government. In fact, Hitler and Veesenmayer were already making plans for just such a takeover.[17]

On October 8, Hungarian representatives delivered Horthy's handwritten letter to Soviet leader Josef Stalin, offering to surrender. Stalin demanded that Hungary give up all of the eastern territories it had gained since 1937 and immediately declare war on the Germans. Horthy had little choice; if he backed down now, Hungary would be crushed by the Soviets. On October 11, he agreed to Stalin's terms.[18]

Change of Plans

Horthy planned to make his official announcement on October 17 or 18. That would give him time to inform his military officers of the agreement, and also time to distribute guns to thousands of workers in Budapest including Jewish laborers in order to stage a rebellion against the Germans. Horthy called for the arrest of the pro-German leaders, including Ferenc Szálasi, the leader of the Arrow Cross. The Germans, however, had discovered Horthy's plan and placed Szálasi under their protection. They also kidnapped one of Horthy's top generals, Szilárd Bakay, who was in charge of the Hungarian troops around Budapest.[19] Horthy made the decision to announce the surrender on October 15.

At 1:00 P.M. on that Sunday afternoon, Hungarians listened to their radios as the Hungarian secretary of state read Regent Horthy's message to his people. The message included the history of Germany's occupation of Hungary and the Gestapo's inhumane treatment of the Jews of Hungary. Horthy explained his decision to surrender to the Soviet Union as follows: "I have decided to safeguard Hungary's honour even against her former ally, although this ally, instead of supplying the promised military help, meant finally to rob the Hungarian nation of its greatest treasure—its freedom and independence." He closed by asking his people to "follow me on this path . . . that will lead to Hungary's salvation."[20]

Tom Lantos was born in 1928 in Budapest, Hungary. Just sixteen years old when the Germans invaded his country, Lantos was captured and sent to a labor camp forty miles north of the city.

After escaping the camp, Lantos returned to Budapest and sought the safety of the Swedish houses run by Raoul Wallenberg. Because of his blonde hair, many people thought Lantos did not look Jewish. Wallenberg acquired a military uniform for Lantos and sent him out to deliver medicine and food to Jews hiding in the city. Lantos risked death on every trip, but he did not expect to survive the war anyway, so he thought, "I might as well be of some use."[21] Lantos was liberated by Russian troops in January 1945.

In 1947, Lantos left Hungary to attend the University of Washington in Seattle. He earned a bachelor's degree and a master's degree, both in economics. Later, Lantos earned a Ph.D. in economics at the University of California in Berkeley. In 1950, he married his Hungarian sweetheart, Annette Tillemann, also rescued by Wallenberg.

Lantos now lives in California and serves the Twelfth District in the United States House of Representatives. He admires Wallenberg because " . . . his conscience did not allow him to remain in that peaceful and secure little island of Sweden. He took a train and joined us in Hell."[22]

The address was repeated twice more. In the Jewish houses, the people celebrated by ripping off their stars and burning them. At the Swedish legation, Lars Berg described the feeling of Wallenberg's staff as, ". . . the deepest and most sincere satisfaction . . . The Hungarian Jews had been saved. This was the end of all deportations, the end of confiscation, ill-treatment, and gas chambers."[23]

They had no way of knowing that this brightest of moments would be followed by the darkest of days for Hungary and its people.

6

The Nyilas
Nightmare
Begins

Celebration in Budapest was quickly followed by confusion. Immediately after Horthy's announcement on October 15, 1944, ended, the radio went silent. Next, it came to life with loud German marches. Through the afternoon and early evening, the Hungarians waited by their radios to learn the fate of their government.

War survivor Laura-Louise Veress lived in the hills near Budapest, where her husband worked in the monitoring service of Hungarian radio.

> All afternoon and evening we kept vigil by the radio, listening with growing apprehension to the military music which filled the time between increasingly confusing proclamations. At twenty minutes after nine in the evening we knew everything was lost when we heard the voice of Ferenc Szálasi, the ruthless leader of the Arrow Cross Party, read out his first "Order of the Day."[1]

Only later would the events of that day become known.

Horthy's Defeat

Horthy's radio announcement had not taken the Germans by surprise. Early that morning, Horthy's son, Miklós Jr., had left the palace for a meeting with Yugoslavian leaders, despite his father's order for him to remain in the palace. A few blocks from home, his car was stopped at a roadblock. He was overpowered and knocked unconscious.

Even as the celebrations were going on in the streets, German tanks moved into Budapest to surround the regent's castle. Plenipotentiary Edmund Veesenmayer, who carried the authority of the German government in Hungary, entered Horthy's office to inform him that his son was being held by the Germans. He must resign his position and turn the government over to Ferenc Szálasi's Nyilas party. Defeated, Horthy agreed to resign and instructed his guards to cooperate with the SS. Veesenmayer assured Horthy that his son would be returned. In fact, young Miklós was already being taken to Mauthausen concentration camp in Germany. He would later be transferred to Dauchau, where he would remain until the Americans liberated the camp at the end of the war. Prime Minister Géza Lakatos also signed over his authority to Szálasi. Horthy went to Germany in the custody of the SS.

Although most Hungarians had no warning of the takeover, some Jewish laborers knew the Arrow Cross had something planned. When László Ernster reported for work at the Arener Street synagogue on October 14, he was surprised to find many new laborers gathered there. The soldiers on guard would not allow the workers to leave or contact their families. They spent that night at the synagogue. The next morning, young men dressed in uniforms of the Arrow Cross guarded the exits. Learning of Horthy's plan to distribute guns to the labor brigades for resistance, the Germans had managed to isolate the Jews to keep watch over them.[2]

Violent Chaos

At the announcement of the Nyilas party takeover, Budapest fell into chaos. The Arrow Cross soldiers used their armbands as a license to kill Jews and steal their property. They invaded both Swiss and Swedish protected houses in the international ghetto, destroyed the passes of the inhabitants, and shot those who resisted. They raided other houses in the Jewish ghetto and killed elderly people. They led Jewish workers at gunpoint to the Danube River, shot them, and let their bodies fall into the river.

A steady stream of anti-Semitic messages came over the radio. They claimed that the Jews were working with the Soviets. Rumors soon spread that the Jews were sending signals to Allied bombers who dropped toys filled with explosives to be picked up by Hungarian children.[3] Many Jews went into hiding. Some were fortunate to have Gentile friends still willing to shelter them.

The situation in the countryside outside Budapest was just as confusing and dangerous. After they learned of Horthy's radio announcement, Hungarian soldiers at the front began handing out guns to the Jews in the labor battalions. "We're on the same side now," they told the Jews.[4] Some soldiers, thinking the war was over, tried to make their way home. At a railroad station just east of Budapest, university student Lajos Takács said that he "spent the afternoon there watching trains traveling west, loaded with jubilant soldiers, coming back from the Eastern Front." When the Nyilas takeover was announced, however, Takács observed the trains going back east again, taking "gloomy-faced soldiers" back to the front.[5]

61

Szálasi's takeover of the government allowed his followers to act out the Nyilas party's hatred of the Jews. At Pusztavám, a small town just west of Budapest, German and Arrow Cross soldiers massacred 216 Jewish laborers. The laborers were professional Jewish men, mostly doctors, pharmacists, and engineers. They were ordered to undress, and then mowed down with machine guns.[6]

October 16 marked the beginning of a living nightmare for the Jews of Budapest, and for Wallenberg as he worked to save them. Szálasi ordered all Jewish houses locked for ten days. During that time, no one would be allowed to leave for food, to seek medical care for the sick, or even to bury the dead. Any Jew caught on the street in Budapest could be shot. Several thousand Jews were arrested and held captive at two large synagogues in central Pest.

In Teleki Square in Pest, a resistance group of Jewish laborers, communists, and socialists attempted an armed revolt against the Arrow Cross. Hungarian police and German SS rushed to the square. The resistance fighters were outnumbered and defeated. In response to the Jewish revolt, the Arrow Cross entered Jewish houses around the square. They took all the occupants into the square and executed them. Hundreds of bodies of men, women, and children were left in the square as a warning to others.[7]

The Disappearance of Section C

When he arrived at his office on October 16, 1944, Wallenberg found the operation of Section C in jeopardy. His entire staff was missing, as were the keys to some locked rooms at the legation. Even his car was gone. Wallenberg found a bicycle in the street and spent the day riding through the city trying to locate his staff members who were hiding and move them to safer quarters.

After he returned to the office, he learned that his driver, Vilmos Langfelder, had been arrested and was being held at Arrow Cross headquarters. Wallenberg acquired another car, and asked Sandor Ardai to drive him there. Waiting in the car outside, Ardai doubted that the Arrow Cross would release Langfelder just because Wallenberg or anyone else demanded it. When Wallenberg emerged with Langfelder, Ardai could hardly believe it. "They jumped into the car and I drove them to the legation," said Ardai. "Nobody commented on what had happened and I started to understand the extraordinary force which was in Raoul Wallenberg."[8]

At the legation office on Üllöi Street, they found that the Arrow Cross had broken into the office, turned over desks, and scattered papers. The soldiers stood, armed and defiant, in the wreckage. Wallenberg stormed into the room, threatening to report them to the Hungarian minister of foreign affairs. "Do you know I'm a foreign diplomat and that you are violating my rights?" he shouted. "Do you know what this means?"[9] The soldiers stepped back and allowed Wallenberg to begin picking up the papers. They soon left. Although the staff feared the men would return later for revenge, they did not.

Szálasi: Hungarian Leader or German Puppet?

The new prime minister and leader of the Arrow Cross party, Ferenc Szálasi, considered himself a Hungarist, a nationalist committed to the welfare of his country. According to Holocaust historian Andrew Handler, "To his followers . . . , he was the embodiment of all human virtues and a Magyar patriot . . . Above all, he was a zealous defender of Hungarian traditions and values and . . . designer of the Hungarist solution, which envisioned a prosperous and peaceful Greater Hungary."[10] Others, however, regarded him as merely a puppet of Adolf Hitler, willing to do all he could to support the Führer.

Whether patriot or puppet, Szálasi's first order of business was to solidify his own position and get Hungary back to the business of handling Hitler's Final Solution. On October 17, he formed a new fifteen-member governing council and publicly declared his opposition to the Soviets and his loyalty to Germany. To gain Hitler's respect, he would need to do what Horthy could not: make Hungary *judenrein*.

Wallenberg to the Rescue

Wallenberg, however, was also ready for action on October 17. He loaded piles of blank Schutz-passes and a typewriter into the back seat of his car and headed to the Dohány Street synagogue. Thousands of Jews had been held captive there for two days with little food or water, in conditions so crowded that they could not even lie down. Wallenberg pushed his way past the Arrow Cross guards into the temple. Standing on the altar, he shouted, "Does anyone here have a Swedish protective pass?" Some held their passes up. Others said that Arrow Cross men had destroyed their passes. Still others recognized the opportunity Wallenberg was giving them and claimed they had lost theirs. Wallenberg formed them into lines and told the guards, "These are all Swedish citizens. You have no right to detain them." They were used to taking orders from German soldiers, and Wallenberg's forceful tone of voice as he confronted them in German took them by surprise. They stood aside as he marched hundreds of Jews out of the synagogue. Using the typewriter in his car, he then typed names on blank passes for those who had no pass.[11]

Conditions for the Jews in Budapest were getting worse each day. Most were still wearing the same clothing they wore the day they had been forced to leave their homes

The new premier of Hungary, Arrow Cross party leader Ferenc Szálasi, greets his troop commander in front of the Ministry of Defense in Budapest. After Horthy's announcement of peace talks with the Soviets, armed Arrow Cross units, with German assistance, took control of strategic positions within the capital.

months before. In many of the houses, people were living twenty or thirty per room. The advance of Soviet troops was causing food shortages in the city. By the time the Jews would be allowed to leave to go to the food markets, it was clear that most of the markets would have no more food of any kind.

65

The food Wallenberg had stockpiled in the previous weeks was now a necessity, since Jews were locked into their houses. He organized six secret warehouses of food and supplies: three on the Buda side of the city, three in Pest. Wallenberg spent most of his time delivering supplies to those in the ghettos and to others who were in hiding. He began wearing hiking boots at all times and carrying his backpack with a change of clothing and some food, just in case he was unable to get back to his home or office.

On October 17, Adolf Eichmann returned to Hungary and called the Jewish Council together for a meeting. "As you can see, I am back. My arm is still long enough to reach you."[12] On October 18, Interior Minister Gábor Vajna made a public announcement that the new government would be handling the solution of the Jewish question and that its solution would be "what the Jews deserve by reason of their previous and present conduct."[13] The Hungarian government would no longer recognize the conversion of any Jews to the Lutheran, Catholic, or other faiths; all Jews would only be recognized as members of the Jewish race. Nor would the government recognize any papers granting safe passage or passports to Hungarian Jews from the government of other nations. Wallenberg's passes were now meaningless.

An Unexpected Ally

The same day Vajna announced the new policy, Wallenberg's phone rang. Karl Müller, a Hungarian Jew who ran a publishing company in Hungary, had also been helping Wallenberg's Section C in Budapest. Müller had received special consideration from Horthy because of his service during World War I, so he was not forced to give up his business or move into the ghetto. He was calling to arrange a meeting for Wallenberg with Baroness Elizabeth Kemény, wife of the Hungarian foreign minister in the new Arrow Cross government. Gábor Kemény was a fierce anti-Semite loyal to Szálasi, but his wife was the daughter of an Austrian baron. At the time they married, she did not know of his association with Hungary's Arrow Cross. She had asked Müller to arrange a meeting with Wallenberg to see how she could help. Perhaps the baroness was motivated by a humanitarian desire to save the Jews. Some historians have suggested that she was herself of Jewish birth.[14] However, the baroness denied this, even many years later.[15]

Wallenberg and the baroness met at Müller's publishing house an hour later.

He was blunt with her. "This Hungarian government is doomed. The Allies have already promised to hold war crimes trials. Your husband and the other Arrow Cross leaders will be executed."[16] Although she disliked the Arrow Cross party, she did not want her husband killed. She was pregnant with his child. Wallenberg's solution to her dilemma would not be easy: She must convince her husband to change the government's position on protective passes for Jews. She promised Wallenberg she would try.

Although Baron Kemény hated the Jews, he loved his wife. He also knew that Szálasi was desperate for international recognition of his new government. On October 20, Kemény met with the Arrow Cross leadership. Kemény suggested that honoring the protective passes would win the favor of the neutral countries and gain the Nyilas party its proper respect as a legitimate government. Later that day, Kemény made a radio announcement ordering all officers to respect the passports of the neutral countries. The holders of the passes would no longer be required to wear the yellow star, they would not be drafted into labor service, and the

67

protected houses displaying the flags of neutral countries would be respected as international territory. It was an important victory for Wallenberg, but was it already too late?

Labor Draft

On the morning of October 20, before Kemény's radio announcement, Arrow Cross men began invading Jewish houses. They took all Jewish men between the ages of sixteen and sixty for labor service, regardless of their physical condition, handicaps, or foreign passports. The men were gathered in the streets, robbed of any valuables, marched to a nearby sports arena, and divided into labor companies to dig trenches and build fortifications at the outskirts of Budapest.

The following day, the labor draft was expanded to include all adult women except those who were pregnant or had infants. Within six days, this new labor force had grown to include over thirty-five thousand people.[17] They were given no warm clothing, coats, shoes, or uniforms—just a yellow armband with the Star of David. Those who could not walk fast enough to keep up with their company or perform the required labor were shot or tortured to death by the guards. Others starved or died of exhaustion or exposure to the cold within a few days.

Wallenberg and the Arrow Cross

In order to protect the Jews from the Arrow Cross, Wallenberg had to know with whom he was dealing. Among the Arrow Cross militia members, some were simply fanatical anti-Semites. They were more concerned with destroying the Jews than with their loyalty to Hungary or to the Nyilas party. Many came from the lower class of Hungarian society and resented the wealth and privileges that others, including some Jews, had enjoyed before the war.

Their newfound authority in the Arrow Cross offered them the opportunity to take out their hatred in unspeakably cruel acts without fear of punishment. There was little discipline among these soldiers, and they often ignored the orders of their superiors. They were quick to shoot any Jew suspected of the smallest violation.[18]

Fortunately for Wallenberg, many of them were illiterate. When Wallenberg appeared and asked for Jews to show their passports, the Arrow Cross soldiers could not tell the difference between a real protective pass, a baptismal certificate, a driver's license, or a written receipt from a store. Their confusion gave Wallenberg the chance to intimidate them with threats in German. It was one thing to violate the rights of the Jews they considered subhuman. It was far different to violate the rights of this man who claimed to represent a foreign government.

Other Arrow Cross men were more moderate. They were easily swayed by Wallenberg's threats to report them to their superior officers and also realized that once the Soviets arrived, as they surely would, they could be prosecuted by the Allies as war criminals. Even more importantly, they were hungry. As the Soviet troops neared Budapest, supply lines coming into the city were cut off. Wallenberg's secret stockpiles of supplies became useful in getting Arrow Cross soldiers to look the other way as he worked to save lives.

Invasions of Jewish houses sometimes turned into bloodbaths. Jews taken from their homes were directed to take only what they could carry. Once out of their houses, they were frequently robbed of these few possessions, as well as their warm coats. As laborers were marched across the bridges over the Danube River, some were shot as they struggled to keep up, some were pushed with a rifle butt, and some

"Tommy" Lapid

At age 13, Tommy Lapid thought he would be an orphan. His father had already been taken to a concentration camp. Then, the Arrow Cross came to take his mother away.

Lapid was born Tomislav Lampel in 1932, in the town of Nvai Sad, Yugoslavia, an area controlled by Hungary. When the Germans invaded Hungary in 1944, they arrested local Jewish leaders, including Tommy's father, Bela Lampel. He was sent to Mauthausen concentration camp, where he died. Tommy's mother was visiting relatives in Budapest at the time, and arranged to have her son sent to her. They moved to a crowded house in the Jewish ghetto.[19]

From their house near the Danube, they had heard the gunfire of Arrow Crossmen shooting Jews. When the soldiers invaded their house, Tommy's mother and the other women were taken. Tommy and his mother cried and hugged, certain they would never see each other again. Several hours later, he was amazed when she returned with the other women. "It seemed like a mirage, a miracle," he said. "My mother was there—she was alive and she was hugging me and kissing me, and she said one word: 'Wallenberg.'"[20]

After the war, Lapid and his mother moved to Tel Aviv, Israel. As of 2004, Lapid was a leader of Israel's Shinui political party, and served as the Israeli Deputy Prime Minister and Justice Minister.

jumped from the bridges to their deaths in the icy river to escape their suffering.

Fortunately, even some Arrow Cross men were shocked at the violence they witnessed. Some Arrow Cross officers decided to help the Jews. They found ways to communicate and cooperate with Wallenberg and other rescuers. According to Holocaust historian Andrew Handler, "Without their promises and acts of cooperation, the work of even men of conspicuous courage and unabating resolve, like Raoul Wallenberg, would have become extremely difficult, if not impossible, yielding few positive results."[21]

Despite the chaos and tragedy surrounding him, Wallenberg found the situation energizing. In a letter to his mother on October 22, he described the situation in Budapest as, ". . . extraordinarily exciting and nerve-racking." He wrote by candlelight because of a power outage and told her, "Dozens of people are standing around me, everyone with pressing questions, so that I don't know to whom to reply and advise first."[22]

To protect more people, Wallenberg added more staff. He recruited more young Jewish men and women, and his staff grew to about four hundred. The Jews on his staff were supposed to be exempt from the labor draft and other actions against the Jews, but the Arrow Cross did not care about a Jew's protected status when they invaded a home. In his letter of October 22 to his home office in Stockholm, Wallenberg reported that he was working to find special housing for them, in order to keep them out of the reach of the Arrow Cross.[23] To do this, he added more houses and opened another office.

Death Marches

As Wallenberg increased his efforts to save the Jews, Adolf Eichmann developed his latest plan to destroy them.

To maintain their war effort, the Germans had stopped Eichmann's deportation plan in August by insisting that trains within Hungary transport troops and supplies, not Jews. Now Eichmann had a new way to get rid of the Jews. Instead of putting them on trains at the stations in Budapest, he would simply make them walk 125 miles from Budapest to a train station at Hegyeshalom, on the Hungarian-Austrian border. There they would be loaded onto trains and sent to their final destinations.

On October 26, the Nyilas minister of defense, Károly Beregfy, announced that Hungary would send seventy labor companies to Germany to replace the "worn out" Soviet prisoners working there. In reality, many of the Soviet prisoners had died of exhaustion and starvation. Those drafted would have to walk from Budapest to Hegyeshalom. The new draft would include virtually all Jews who had not already been assigned to labor companies. Most of the Jews still in Budapest had been judged too old, too young, or too sick to work in the labor battalions drafted on October 20. Few could be expected to make it to Hegyeshalom alive. The movements of these masses along the roads to Hungary's borders would be known as the "death marches." Eliminating the last of Hungary's Jews would be Eichmann's greatest victory. Saving them would become Wallenberg's biggest challenge so far.

7

Marched to Death

On the first of November, Raoul Wallenberg and Swiss consul Carl Lutz were called to a meeting with Baron Kemény. Each day since October 20, Wallenberg and Lutz had appeared in Teleki Square where the daily roundup of Jews for the labor draft took place. Every day they called out for those who had protective passes to step out of line, and every day they saved hundreds of people. Now that the Nyilas had agreed to recognize their passports, Kemény wanted to know when the neutral countries would officially recognize the Nyilas government. He also asked when these Swedish and Swiss citizens would be leaving Hungary. He would give them until the end of November to remove their citizens; after that they would be treated like all other Jews.

Besides the difficulty of arranging transportation during wartime for thousands of people, there were other problems to consider. Once the protected Jews and the foreign diplomats were gone, the remaining Jews would be defenseless.

Also, there would be no guarantee of the safety of those Jews traveling out of Hungary. What would prevent the Nazis from attacking a train or other transport of Jews?

Wallenberg responded to Kemény's threat with a list of questions: How many days apart should the convoys be scheduled? Would the travelers be allowed to take food? Should they report to local authorities before leaving? Kemény had no answers. With a month until Kemény's deadline, the diplomats hoped that the Soviet advance would make all arrangements unnecessary. If pressed again for the deportation of the protected Jews, Wallenberg would again demand answers to his questions.[1]

The Soviets were close at hand. On November 2, they broke through the German and Hungarian defenses just southeast of Budapest. Soviet troops advanced within eight miles of the city. Arrow Cross soldiers supervising Jewish labor battalions outside the city blamed the Jews for the loss and killed many who could not keep up with them as they went back into the city. They forced hundreds of the workers to march onto the bridges over the Danube, then shot them and let the bodies fall into the river. Hungarian police were called in to protect the Jews from their guards.

The nearer the Soviets came to Budapest, the more desperate Szálasi became to destroy the Jews, or at least to make life more miserable for them. Wallenberg always tried to be one step ahead of the Arrow Cross. One day the Arrow Cross went into Jewish houses and seized the food ration cards of all the Jews. Szálasi then issued a decree that anyone without a ration card would be deported. Wallenberg and his staff responded by printing their own ration cards that stated that the bearer would be supplied food by Section C. Next Szálasi declared that only passports from the neutral countries would be valid to exempt a Jew from labor service, not protective passes. Wallenberg prepared and signed notes to be attached to the passes saying that each protective pass was valid for use as a Swedish passport. As the Soviets came nearer the city, Wallenberg had passes printed in Russian and made identifying signs for the protected houses with their messages in Russian as well.[2]

Dangerous Adversary

By now, Wallenberg had become so effective at saving the Jews that Adolf Eichmann became concerned that he would interfere with his plan to march the Jews to Hegyeshalom. Wallenberg and the other neutral diplomats sent protests to the Hungarian government to prevent the marches. Eichmann summoned Wallenberg to meet him at the Hotel Majestic. "You're a Jew-lover who's received all his dirty dollars from Roosevelt!" Eichmann accused. "We also know all about your so-called passports. They're all frauds." Wallenberg offered Eichmann some whiskey. After a few drinks he calmed down. "Let me do you a favor," the German offered. "If you want, and of course the price is right—say seven hundred and fifty thousand Swiss francs—I would be happy to put a train at your disposal. You could then take all your protected Jews to Sweden. What do you say?"[3]

Wallenberg agreed to think about it. Even if Eichmann would provide a train, which seemed impossible, Wallenberg could not go back to Sweden with a few thousand Jews and leave the rest to face the brutality of the Arrow Cross. The marches of Jews to the Hungarian border would start soon, and he must stay to do whatever he could. He knew that the worst was soon to come.

The Death Marches Begin

November 8, 1944, was the official day for the beginning of the marches. As the Arrow Cross went from one ghetto building to the other to gather their victims, they paid the building superintendents to provide them with lists of the people who lived there, just to be sure they did not miss anyone. Several places in Budapest, including the brick factory in Obuda, were designated as gathering points for the marchers before they began their journey. There they were counted and kept for several days until the march began. They were given little if any food or water and had to sleep in the open or in the brick-drying barn that had a roof but no walls to protect them from the cold November weather. Blankets, coats, and all valuables were taken by the Arrow Cross guards, leaving the marchers with virtually nothing.[4]

Wallenberg and Lutz again came to help the suffering people. They made daily trips to the brickyard to rescue those with protective papers. Wallenberg now had a regular method for these rescues: He carried a folding table in his car, along with a typewriter, blank passes, and his "Book of Life" that supposedly listed the names of Jews with protective passes, although often it had only blank pages or simply lists of common Jewish names.

Stephen Lazarovitz, a medical intern, was taken to the brickyard. When Wallenberg appeared that day, the Arrow Cross guard called for all those with Swedish passes to step forward but warned that if any stepped forward without passes, they would be executed on the spot. Lazarovitz had a forged pass. He decided to step forward anyway, and took his place near the end of the line. After an hour of waiting, he was near the table. He recognized a friend who was working for Wallenberg and whispered his problem. The friend told Wallenberg. When Lazarovitz approached the table, Wallenberg took the forged pass and announced, "I remember this doctor. I gave him his passport personally. Let's not waste our time because it's late. We need him now at the Emergency Hospital of the Swedish embassy." The Nazi officer echoed, "Let's not waste our time! Next."[5] Many were not so lucky as Lazarovitz. On the first day of the roundup, over ten thousand Jews were taken for the marches.[6]

Life and Death in the Brickyards

Those held at the Obuda brickyards endured the most inhumane conditions imaginable. According to Susan Tabor, a survivor of the experience, "There was no light, no water, no food, no doctors, no first aid, no sanitary facilities, no one was allowed outside. Armed Nazis walked around stepping on people, abusing them, cursing and shooting. We were beaten. Our spirit was broken."[7] As they were led into the brickyard in the dark, some people fell into holes in the floor and were trampled by the hundreds of others who followed.

One morning Wallenberg arrived at the brickyard and, using a megaphone, he spoke to them from outside the gate. "I will bring you food and water. Doctors and nurses will be with you shortly. Don't give up hope. I will return for anyone with a Swedish passport."[8] A few hours later, he returned with the medical help. The next day he arrived with Swiss consul Carl Lutz and a convoy of trucks. He saved five hundred women from the march, choosing girls and younger women. He apologized to those he left behind, explaining that he must choose the young in order to save the Jewish nation. They climbed onto the trucks for the trip back to the Jewish protected houses.

Columns of Jewish marchers walked the road from Budapest, on the 125-mile trip to Hegyeshalom, near the

Austrian border. Because so many adults had already been sent for labor service, many of the remaining victims were children younger than sixteen, pregnant women, the elderly, or those who had previously been rejected because they were judged to be unfit for labor. The neutral diplomats who witnessed the brutal treatment of the marchers were horrified. Lars Berg, one of Wallenberg's colleagues at the Swedish legation, reported:

> It was horrible to have to be standing as a passive spectator when young girls were driven together, arranged in files and sent off, dressed in silk stockings, high-heeled shoes, and thin office clothes. Together with them were old people who would hardly be able to make the first mile without falling.[9]

Long Road to Hegyeshalom

Although the marchers were supposedly headed for labor in Austria, many would never make it to the border. Those who stumbled or fell were shot by the guards. Some of the elderly had heart attacks. Others collapsed from exhaustion and hunger. They had no food, water, or warm clothing. The lucky ones were given some thin soup every few days. The roadside from Budapest to Hegyeshalom was lined with the bodies of those whose misery had ended. Many mornings the marchers awoke to find bodies of suicide victims hanging from trees. When one group stopped overnight next to the Danube, some of them jumped into the icy river to end their suffering.[10]

The brutality of the Arrow Cross guards on the marches was so horrifying that even some of the Nazi officials and Hungarian gendarmes complained. Hans Jüttner, a Nazi general, called the situation "truly terrifying," and wanted to know who had ordered these atrocities. He was informed that Adolf Eichmann was responsible.[11] Although many of the Hungarian officers cooperated, some of them found it sickening. Some soldiers assigned to escort the marchers refused and demanded to be sent back to the war's front.

Wallenberg, Lutz, and Per Anger made many trips on the road from Budapest to Hegyeshalom. They loaded their cars with food and medical supplies for the marchers they passed. According to Anger, "We passed those masses of unfortunates, more dead than alive. Ashy-faced, they staggered forward under the prodding and blows from the soldiers' rifle butts. The road was edged with bodies."[12] It was illegal to give aid to the Jews, but cognac and cigarettes often persuaded guards to look away.

Those who survived the march would have to face Eichmann, who waited at the station. As Wallenberg raced toward the train station, he made his plans for saving those who were about to fall into Eichmann's hands. Fourteen-year-old Zvi Eres marched toward the station in a group with his mother, his aunt, and a cousin. Along the road they saw a car stopped ahead of them, and a man introduced himself as a Swedish diplomat and asked if any of them had Swedish passports or if their passports had been taken by the Arrow Cross. According to Eres, "We were on our last legs, but alert enough to take the hint and we said, yes, that was exactly what had happened, though in fact none of us had ever had a Swedish *Schutzpass*. He put our names on a list and we walked on."[13] At the station, Wallenberg produced the list and demanded that they be released. Nearly three hundred people were saved that day.[14]

Eichmann's Threats

Eichmann did not take this interference lightly. He was counting Jews at the station. "The main thing is the statistics," he told his deputy, Dieter Wisliceny. "Every Jew must be accounted for."[15] As Wallenberg and the other diplomats

An American soldier looks at the corpses of Polish, Russian, and Hungarian Jews found in the woods near Neunburg vorm Wald. The victims were prisoners from Flossenbuerg who were shot near Neunburg while on a death march.

continued pulling Jews out of the march, Eichmann became more angry. A Red Cross worker overheard him exclaim, "I'm going to kill that Jew-Dog Wallenberg!"[16] One night, an SS truck ran into Wallenberg's car at full speed. Fortunately, Wallenberg was using a different car that night.

Wallenberg's photographer, Tom Veres, recalled that they frequently changed the license plates and window stickers on Wallenberg's car to avoid being stopped and questioned. Despite the danger, Wallenberg kept his sense of humor.

80

"One day our car was in heavy artillery fire and there was our car with one license plate in front, a different license plate in the back . . ." Wallenberg jokingly remarked, "We should get an automatic gadget so that when one license plate appears the others will disappear."[17] In fact, Raoul Wallenberg seemed to thrive on the danger and excitement of these days. According to historian Andrew Handler, "It was in the circumstances of challenge, intrigue, and danger that Wallenberg was in his element."[18]

More Threats Against the Jews

November 15 brought a new order from Szálasi: All protected Jews must move to yellow-star houses in a designated area of Pest. The houses would be specifically identified and segregated for those holding passes from Sweden, Switzerland, Portugal, Spain, the Catholic Church, or the Red Cross and would now form a condensed international ghetto. For the next several days, thousands of Jews moved their few remaining belongings on carts through the streets to their assigned houses. Many of them were stopped by the Arrow Cross who stole their possessions, took them for torture at Arrow Cross headquarters, or just killed them in the street.

On November 19, Baron Kemény revealed the newest threat to Hungarian Jewry. Kemény told Wallenberg's friend Karl Müller that the Nyilas government was tired of waiting for the recognition of the neutral nations and had planned a pogrom to get rid of the Jews. "If Stockholm doesn't recognize our government by November twenty-second then I'll hand all the Jews in Budapest over to Interior Minister Vajna," he threatened. "It means they'll all be drowned in the Danube, and on November twenty-second, Budapest will be *judenrein*."[19] He instructed Müller to inform Wallenberg. Wallenberg went to Vajna to delay the pogrom but was

Tom Veres

Tom Veres was born in 1923 in Budapest. When the Germans invaded Hungary he was sent to a labor camp, but later escaped. Veres knew Per Anger, so he went to the Swedish legation to seek help. Anger thought Veres' photography skills could be useful to the rescue mission. Veres began taking identification photos for Schutz-passes. On November 28, 1944, Veres received a note from Wallenberg that said, "Meet me at Josefvarosi Station. Bring your camera."[20] When Veres arrived, thousands of Jewish prisoners were inside cattle cars to be taken to a death camp. Wallenberg was pulling prisoners from the train and issuing Schutz-passes.

Veres knew he could be killed if he were caught taking pictures. He cut a hole in his heavy scarf and slipped his camera into it. He walked through the crowd, snapping photos with his camera hidden in his scarf. In this way, Veres created a photographic record of the Hungarian deportations and of Wallenberg's work.

Veres narrowly escaped capture along with Wallenberg, and felt an obligation to tell his story. Said Veres, "All I can tell you is that his weapons were his wits, determination, and a belief in the worth of each human life to the point of risking his own in exchange."[21]

In 1956, Veres emigrated to the United States. He died July 23, 2002.

unsuccessful. Next, he went back to reason with Kemény. Eventually, he and Müller convinced the baron to wait until December 14. They believed Soviets would control the city by then.

Gentile Attitudes

The daily roundup of Jews for the death marches continued. As the crowds of marchers made their way toward the brick factory, some of their Gentile neighbors openly jeered at them. Others simply turned away as Jewish marchers passed. Through their propaganda, the Germans convinced many Hungarians that the anti-Jewish measures were in the best interests of the country and that it was their patriotic duty to report infractions.[22]

Some Gentiles were forced to move from their homes in the city that were turned into yellow-star houses in the expanding Jewish ghetto. Still others had benefited by taking over the vacated houses or businesses of Jews who had moved into the ghetto. The Arrow Cross also rewarded those who helped in the persecution of the Jews. Those who reported Jews who had broken curfew or were observed looking out the windows of their houses were rewarded with valuables stolen from Jews. Those who were caught aiding or sheltering Jews could be severely punished. Some were even forced to join the death marches with their Jewish neighbors.

Despite the propaganda encouraging them to hate the Jews, some Hungarians still risked their own lives to help. Some did so by hiding Jewish families in their homes or by taking food to those in the ghetto. Others openly objected to the cruelty of the Arrow Cross. Miriam Herzog reported that as her group walked along the road to Hegyeshalom, a man came out of a house to bring water to them. "The gendarmes tried to stop him," she said, "but he just fixed them with a stare. 'I'd like to see you try to make me,' he said—and went on giving us water. The gendarmes were so amazed, they did nothing about it."[23]

Daring Diplomat

Wallenberg continued giving aid to the marchers and trying to rescue more people. Sometimes, when he saw dying women clutching young children, he would stop and pick up the children and place them on the floor of his car to take them to the children's houses in Budapest.[24]

Eichmann and his staff waited at the train station, counting off the Jews who arrived and overseeing the transfer of the prisoners to the Germans. Wallenberg took advantage of the fact that Eichmann's men could not read Hungarian. He often called out for those who had proof that they had ever received a pass to step forward. Those who understood the trick dug in their pockets for any scrap of paper with a name on it: a driver's license, a ration card, a receipt. Wallenberg examined each one seriously and had his assistant add the name to his list and type the information on a Schutz-pass.

Some days, Wallenberg would arrive at the station with a group of SS officers, Arrow Cross men, or Red Cross volunteers. He had managed to purchase these uniforms through the underground or through bribery and chose fair-haired young people from the Jewish youth underground group, *Halutzim*, to impersonate these officials to lend more authority to his rescue efforts.[25] Eighteen-year-old Kate Lebovitz worked for the *Halutzim*, carrying false Red Cross identification. She also had a certificate of baptism that identified her as a Catholic. According to Kate and her husband Eugene, who also worked for the *Halutzim*, they were not allowed to know more than two or three other people in the organization. "It was dangerous to know too much," said Eugene. "We could be captured and tortured to tell them about the operation." Kate Lebowitz added, "You never knew if it would be your last day, your last minute."[26]

Living Conditions in the International Ghetto

Those rescued by the diplomats were not out of danger. They were returned to the protected houses in the international ghetto. The houses were becoming more crowded and more threatened every day. About fifteen thousand Jews had genuine protective passes from the Swiss, Swedish, Portuguese, and Spanish legations, as well as those protected by the Catholic Church. Many thousands more had forged passes. They were living in apartments that had previously held fewer than four thousand people.[27]

On November 26, Swiss diplomat Carl Lutz submitted a report describing the conditions. "All the protected houses . . . are overcrowded to such an extent that part of the people accommodated in them are obliged to live in the staircases, corridors, and cellars . . . For five days the inhabitants had no food at all, and very little afterwards."[28] Lutz went on to describe raids by the Arrow Cross and Hungarian police in which food was stolen, protective passes taken and re-sold, and bribes demanded. He also reported that many of the Jews in the houses were ill.[29]

An End to the Marches

Eichmann, however, was very pleased. He was receiving praise from the Reich for his accomplishments. According to the report of the rural police, 76,209 Hungarian Jews had been delivered to the Germans for labor in the days between November 6 and December 1.[30] At least another ten thousand people had died before they ever reached Hegyeshalom.[31] Heinrich Himmler had ordered the gas chambers at

85

Auschwitz destroyed, but that was of little concern. After all, the gas chamber just shortened the suffering of those killed that way. Eichmann knew that few Jews would survive the work, cold, and hunger of the concentration camps.

The Nyilas leaders in Budapest arranged a party in Eichmann's honor. He proudly recounted, "[Hungarian General] Winkelmann congratulated me on the 'elegant performance.' So did Veesenmayer. So did Endre."[32] When Eichmann learned that the railroad tracks leading into Austria had been bombed and could no longer take the Jews from Hegyeshalom to the concentration camps, he was not concerned. After all, they had walked this far—they could just continue on and walk the rest of the way to the camps.

Eichmann's plan did not continue much longer, however. The SS troops at the Austrian border were unhappy about the many Jews being sent to them for labor who were so starved and weak that they were barely alive, and certainly not suitable for work. Although the Austrians did not want to accept them, the Hungarians would not take them back. Rudolf Höss, the Nazi commander of Auschwitz, was now in charge of Jewish labor in Austria. He announced that he would only accept able-bodied workers, and he preferred men under age forty.[33]

By the end of November, the prolonged brutality of the death marches was becoming international knowledge. Wallenberg and the other neutral diplomats continued to file official objections with the Hungarian government and were also sending reports back to their home countries about the atrocities being committed. Szalási, still hoping to gain the respect of foreign governments, announced that the marches would end, although they would continue to use Hungarian Jews for labor for Germany. Also, women would no longer walk to the border, but would have to be transported by train or truck.

Eichmann had to come up with a new way to complete the annihilation of the Budapest Jews. Within just a few days he had found it. He ordered the Jewish labor battalions to begin a new project: building a six-foot-high fence around the Jewish ghetto. Once completed, the Jews would be confined within a small area. And now, the protected Jews would have no way out, either. He planned to force them to move into the new ghetto. Wallenberg would have to begin a new battle.

Unholy Nights

Eichmann now had to find a new way to continue his deportations. Only one group of Jewish men left in Budapest fit Höss's requirement that laborers be healthy men: the Swedish labor battalions Wallenberg had gained protection for during September. Although he could no longer march them to Hegyeshalom, Eichmann had received permission to use the rail line from Budapest.

Wallenberg received a tip one morning about the deportation of a Swedish labor battalion and raced to the station to stop it. He managed to intimidate the young SS trooper in charge and rescued three hundred laborers. The next day, however, Eichmann was ready for him. Instead of the usual SS trooper in charge, Eichmann assigned a senior officer, Captain Theodor Dannecker, to oversee the loading of prisoners at the station that day. When Dannecker spotted Wallenberg, he drew his pistol, cursed at him, and chased him from the station.[1]

When he complained to the local head of the SS, Theodore Grell, that his diplomatic immunity had been violated, he was told he should ". . . worry more about the real Swedes living in Budapest. These Jews aren't Swedes. However, if you insist on becoming involved in things that don't concern you, then I cannot, unfortunately, protect you from the consequences."[2] In early December, Wallenberg sent a letter to his home office in Stockholm. He noted that his department had been able to rescue a total of about two thousand people from deportation since the beginning of November, but added, "This practice has unfortunately had to cease after the Germans in the Eichmann Command threatened violent action."[3]

Fencing in the Ghetto

Meanwhile, the Jewish laborers still in Budapest were busy with Eichmann's next phase of persecution of the Jews: building a six-foot wooden fence around the main Jewish ghetto in Pest. There would be only four gates, and all would be guarded. Once inside, no Jews would be permitted to leave. The fence enclosed an area equal to one tenth of a square mile, about the same as ten city blocks in an American city. The Hungarian government said the plan was to prevent a Jewish uprising. Wallenberg and the other neutral diplomats worried that the Nyilas Party planned to keep the Jews confined to make it easier to destroy them all before the Soviets could liberate them.

Szálasi's plan called for about sixty-three thousand Jews to live in the two hundred buildings in the ghetto, but many more would eventually be held there. To make room for them, twelve thousand Gentiles were forced to move out of the area into former yellow-star houses that were now vacant.[4] The Arrow Cross again took advantage of the opportunity to rob, torture, and kill Jews who were moving their few belongings through the streets.

The senseless violence was hard for Wallenberg to bear. Wallenberg was powerless to stop the continued deportation of the Swedish labor brigades and the attacks on those forced to move into the ghetto. In the early morning hours of December 4, the bodies of hundreds of men from the labor brigades were dumped from trucks into the streets. All had been shot in the back of the neck.[5]

A Hungarian staff member of the Red Cross arrived at Wallenberg's office one day to find him sitting in the dark, unshaven and depressed. Wallenberg went to the window and pointed to the street below. "Every minute there is something to see down there," he said. "And if not there, somewhere else. Even while we speak, somewhere, someone else is being murdered by the Arrow Cross . . . Laws no longer exist here; anything can happen."[6]

Living in a War Zone

The Soviet siege of Budapest began December 8. Although the Soviets were ready to take the city, the German and Hungarian troops were determined to hold it. However, the defeat of the Nazis seemed certain. Instead of sending troops into the city, the Soviets began firing artillery into the heart of the city. Soviet planes flew overhead, dropping bombs on the city.

By the following day, the Soviets had advanced on the north, east, and south edges of the city. The only way out of Budapest was to the west. As they advanced, the retreating Germans continued their atrocities against the Jews. Laura-Louise Veress and her family lived just outside the city. A former nursing home on their street had been turned into a house where Jews were held. "We could only imagine what was going on inside," said Veress. "After the siege we found out, as we watched work crews remove piles of charred bodies and haul them away by the wagon load. Before abandoning the area to the Soviets, the Nazis had locked up the [house] and set it on fire."[7]

For the Jews inside the central ghetto, the siege of the city carried the hope of liberation, but it also increased their miseries. At the beginning of December, daily rations for each Jewish person in the ghetto were decreased to a daily diet of about seven hundred calories. Under Hungarian law, inmates in prisons were given fifteen hundred calories per day. Many times the Jews did not even receive the rations they were allowed. As the city was bombed, deliveries were canceled. Often, the Arrow Cross guards at the ghetto gates would not allow the deliveries to come through.[8]

Most buildings in the ghetto had no water. The only fuel for heat came from wood gathered from bombed-out buildings. Those brave enough to go out on the street went to other buildings to bring back water for drinking and cooking. In many houses, the drinking water was kept in the bathtubs, so bathing was impossible. The combination of cold, hunger, and disease due to poor sanitation took many lives.

Rescuers in Action

In the midst of this despair, Wallenberg, the Red Cross, and the underground Zionist youth *Halutzim* combined forces to bring a measure of relief. Wallenberg moved from the relative safety of the Buda district into Pest to be nearer the ghetto and the protected houses. Friedrich Born of the Red Cross recruited a British-educated Hungarian Jew, George Wilhelm, to lead a daring rescue campaign. Wilhelm spoke excellent German and acquired a black uniform like those worn by high-ranking SS officers. He assembled a team of twenty-five men clad in Nazi uniforms. Wilhelm and his men carried out daring raids on houses where Jews were being held, demanding their release into his "custody." In this way, he took hundreds to safety.[9]

The Red Cross lent ambulances to the members of the *Halutzim* to rescue those who were ill and get them to medical care, which was outlawed within the ghetto. Two hospitals outside the ghetto operated under the protection of the Red Cross. In addition to those who were sick, people who were hoping for protection from the Arrow Cross crowded the hospitals. Despite the overcrowding and the lack of drugs and disinfectants, the hospitals were still the best hope for the very ill.[10]

Kate and Eugene Lebovitz were among those who helped with this rescue effort. They carried false Red Cross identification and drove ambulances through the ghetto gates where they were checked by Arrow Cross soldiers. It was dangerous work, but Kate's light-colored hair and fair complexion, combined with her false papers, helped her play the role. Eighteen-year-old Kate had to keep her involvement in the *Halutzim* secret. "Even my mother never knew what we were doing," she said. "It would be too dangerous for all of us."[11]

Arrow Cross Torture

Those caught assisting rescue efforts were sometimes taken to Arrow Cross headquarters for interrogation and torture. The Arrow Cross had many methods of torture. In some cases, the eyes of victims were burned out with hot nails. In one Arrow Cross torture room, Jews were beaten with leather straps and forced to clean toilets with their tongues. An examination of the corpses of Jewish victims by the Budapest Institute of Forensic Medicine reported that most had suffered prolonged agony before death. According to historian

Harvey Rosenfeld, "From the distorted faces of the corpses the conclusion could be drawn that their sufferings had been ghastly . . . Shooting out of eyes, scalping, deliberate breaking of bones, and abdominal knife wounds were Nyilas specialties."[12] Kate Lebovitz was captured by the Arrow Cross and taken to one of their buildings. She managed to escape, but not before being forced to watch several Arrow Cross men torture a fifty-five-year-old Gentile woman who was being interrogated.[13]

Conditions in the international ghetto were not much better than those in the main ghetto. Wallenberg's letter to Stockholm on December 8 reported that seven thousand people were living in the Swedish houses, twenty-three thousand in Swiss-protected houses, and another two thousand in houses run by the Red Cross. He also reported that raids on houses protected by the Swiss and the Catholics had caused thousands to be taken to the deportation areas or moved to the main ghetto.[14] Because the Swiss protective passes had been the easiest to copy, there were actually more counterfeit than authentic Swiss passes in circulation in Budapest. Because of this, the Swiss houses became easy targets for the Arrow Cross.

International Politics

Relations between the Swedish legation and the Nyilas government became more strained as each day passed. After a raid on the Red Cross headquarters in which staff members were arrested and ordered to cease all operations, Per Anger and other members of the legation made a protest to the Hungarian Foreign Ministry. They were not received kindly. The Hungarian diplomat in Stockholm, Ladislas Vöczköndy, had recently been ordered to leave Sweden because he was a member of the Arrow Cross party.[15] According to Anger, the action of the Swedish government endangered the legation's mission and especially placed Wallenberg in danger.[16]

Wallenberg decided it was time to once again face his opponent: He invited Eichmann to dinner. They dined with some other Swedes and a deputy of Eichmann's. After the meal, the group sat down in the living room for drinks and conversation. Wallenberg took advantage of the opportunity for dramatics as he turned out the lights and opened the curtains so they could look out over the city as the Soviet bombs and gunfire lit the city with explosions. Wallenberg began to debate with Eichmann the foolishness of Nazism. He pointed out that the war was all but lost for the Germans and that the continuing drive to kill the Jews could only result in Eichmann's execution for his war crimes. According to Lars Berg, Eichmann agreed with Wallenberg's assessment of the situation. "I admit that you are right, Herr Wallenberg. I admit that I have never believed in Nazism as such, but it has given me power and wealth," said Eichmann. "For me there will be no escape, but if I obey my orders from Berlin and exercise my power harshly enough, I may prolong my respite here in Budapest." He finished the conversation with a threat for Wallenberg. "I will do my best to stop you, and your Swedish diplomatic passport will not help you if I find it necessary to have you removed."[17] Wallenberg soon began alternating between two apartments, as well as spending nights in other locations in the city to avoid capture.

On December 16, Minister Gábor Vajna met with deputies of Heinrich Himmler in Berlin to discuss the fate of the Jews of Budapest. Together they decided it was time for Hungary to at last be *judenrein*. According to Vajna's testimony after the war, he was sent back to Budapest with instructions to work out a plan with Eichmann for getting rid of all remaining Jews, using whatever force was needed.[18] Rounding up and executing the Jews in the main ghetto would be a fairly simple matter, but there were still those in the protected houses, the Jewish children in the Red Cross houses called Section A, and thousands more hiding within the city.

Hasty Departure

Christmas week brought a wave of violence and terror to Budapest. On December 22, the Soviets broke through the German defenses just southwest of the city. The city was nearly surrounded now. Eichmann and the rest of the German staff decided it was time to leave Budapest by the last open road, but there was business to take care of first. As the Germans were vacating their offices, they had to consider who would look after the property they were leaving behind. Perhaps they feared Soviet intrusion of the premises; perhaps they simply did not trust the Arrow Cross to guard the building. Although the reason is unclear, the Germans called Minister Carl Ivan Danielsson at the Swedish legation to ask if the legation would take the keys to the building, thus placing it under Swedish protection. Anger was sent to arrange the details. When he arrived, the Germans were busy burning files as they prepared to leave. The Swedes took the keys to the building.[19]

Meanwhile, Eichmann was making his own preparations to leave Budapest. First, he organized an effort to get ammunition to the front lines. He formed a two-mile line of Jews to carry shells from the storage facility to the German and Hungarian soldiers at the front.[20] Next, he called the headquarters of the Jewish Council inside the ghetto. He ordered the Council to gather there to meet with him at 9:00 P.M.

At 9:00 that evening, Eichmann's car arrived at the Jewish Council building. Eichmann, accompanied by two armed officers and a trooper with a submachine gun, approached the door with their weapons drawn. Two other cars of armed troopers arrived. Eichmann pounded on the door, demanding to see the council members. The startled building manager opened the door, insisting that there had been a mistake; he had been told that the council would meet at 9:00 the next morning. Eichmann cursed at the man, threatened to shoot him and his sister, and had the troopers beat the man with the butts of their guns. Meanwhile, the council members were hiding in various locations in the ghetto. Later, they reported that Wallenberg's informants had learned that Eichmann planned to assassinate the council, and Wallenberg had advised them to hide for a few days.[21] Before dawn, Eichmann retreated along the only open road out of Budapest.

Szálasi Governs From Sopron

The Hungarian government was now operating from the town of Sopron in western Hungary. Szálasi, Vajna, and Kemény had all retreated to avoid the advancing Soviet troops. They left the rest of the Arrow Cross and a few officials in charge of carrying out the new anti-Jewish regulations in Budapest. Anger and Wallenberg were called to the office of Ladislas Vöczköndy, the new acting foreign minister. Vöczköndy was still angry at having been forced to leave his diplomatic position in Sweden. He greeted the diplomats coldly. Vöczköndy informed them that, if they chose to remain in Budapest, the Hungarian government would no longer guarantee their safety. He advised them to leave immediately. Anger and Wallenberg discussed the situation and agreed that they could not abandon the protected Jews, nor leave the nearly seventy thousand residents of the main

96

ghetto to the Arrow Cross. They purchased guns to protect themselves.[22]

The Soviet siege brought new decrees against the Jews from the Szálasi government, even though most of its officers were no longer in Budapest. Gábor Vajna ordered all Jews in Budapest to immediately move to the fenced main ghetto. This included those in the protected houses, children in the Section A houses, those hiding in other places, as well as workers at the diplomatic legations living within their buildings.

Because this law made it a crime for any Jew to live outside the ghetto, it touched off a wave of violence more horrifying than any so far. The Arrow Cross preferred to operate under cover of darkness. Each night after December 23 brought new atrocities. Protected houses were invaded, and their inhabitants taken to the banks of the Danube. There, victims were stripped of their clothing and tied together in groups of three. The middle person was then shot in the head or the back, and all three pushed into the icy river. Shocked by the cold water and pulled down by their dead companion, the other two had little chance of surviving. The Arrow Cross said that this technique saved ammunition, but often the soldiers along the banks shot for sport at those in the water.

Terror for Christmas

On December 24, Christmas Eve, Soviets reached the outskirts of Buda. The city was now completely surrounded. The Arrow Cross observed the holiday with even more acts of hatred. At 5:00 A.M., the Swedish legation office was raided, and the staff members kidnapped. Lars Berg and several other staff members were taken. Berg managed to escape his captors and go to the German SS headquarters. He reminded the SS that the Swedes had custody of the keys to the German legation and therefore

97

Agnes Mandl Adachi

Agnes Mandl Adachi was born in Budapest in 1918. In 1944, she moved into one of the Swedish protected houses and worked as a clerk, writing Schutz-passes. Wallenberg sometimes sent the clerks, all of whom were Jewish, out at night to deliver the passes, since the Arrow Cross usually conducted their raids just before dawn. Despite the threat of execution if caught, "It was impossible for us to be afraid with Wallenberg as our leader," she said. " . . . [I]f he could take such risks, then so could we."[23]

One winter night, Wallenberg asked anyone who could swim to join him at the Danube River. Adachi and three men volunteered. At the river bank, Arrow Cross soldiers were tying prisoners in groups of three. They shot the middle person of each group and pushed all three into the river between the floating slabs of ice. Wallenberg and his staff, including medical personnel, parked their cars downstream, out of sight of the Arrow

The Danube River

Cross. Adachi and the other swimmers jumped into the river to rescue the victims as others on shore helped pull them out. They saved fifty people. "But without Raoul Wallenberg," said Adachi, "we wouldn't have saved even one single person."[24]

After the Russians liberated Budapest, Adachi lived first in Romania, then Sweden and later Australia. She moved to the United States in 1951.

should have German protection from the Arrow Cross. The SS officer in charge agreed and gave Berg a document that declared the Swedish legation to be protected by the German Reich. Two women staff members, however, were still missing.[25] Wallenberg was not at the legation. He was working to save the most helpless of the Nazi's victims, the children.

Wallenberg, along with Ottó Komoly of the Red Cross, Giorgio Perlasca and Lászlo Szamosi of the Spanish legation, and other neutral diplomats sent a strongly worded message to the Hungarian foreign minister, protesting the removal of the Jewish children. "Even in war, conscience and the law condemn hostile actions against children," they wrote. "Every civilized nation respects children, and the whole world will be painfully surprised should traditionally Christian and gallant Hungary decide to institute steps against the little ones."[26]

Their letter had no effect on the new policy. Arrow Cross troopers broke into a children's home. They killed toddlers as young as eighteen months and forced others into the Danube to drown. The next evening, Christmas Day, another home was raided. Several children were killed and the remaining children and their teacher marched to the Danube. A Soviet artillery attack interrupted the march and many of the children escaped, but a teacher and at least six children were shot by the Arrow Cross.[27]

Death Brigades

Violence against the Jews continued to increase in the days after Christmas. Arrow Cross "death brigades" roamed the streets, raiding houses both in and out of the ghetto. One of the most notorious of these was led by Father Andras Kun. Dressed in a monk's robe and a gun belt, he accompanied a gang of Arrow Cross troopers as they invaded houses and led groups of people at gunpoint to the banks of the Danube or to mass graves. After the victims were lined up, he held a crucifix up and commanded, "In the holy name of Jesus Christ, fire!"[28]

In the daylight, Budapest had become a horrible sight. Bodies littered the streets and washed up on the shores of the Danube. Blood-stained ice chunks floated down the river. Crumbled and smoking ruins of buildings lined the boulevards. But nighttime was the worst; darkness brought terror. Georg Libik worked on Wallenberg's staff and went with him to help rescue people who had been taken from a Swedish house in an Arrow Cross raid. He described the scene that night: "It was a frightful scene on the streets of Pest. Everywhere there were houses on fire. It was my country, part of my life being destroyed. But with all the human corpses, all the dead horses strewn along the streets, there was no time for meditation."[29]

Wallenberg's Schemes

As Arrow Cross activity increased, Wallenberg became more bold and inventive in his activities to protect the Jews. He dressed young staffers in Arrow Cross uniforms. They would stop and question real Arrow Cross troopers in the streets, challenge their identity, and then confiscate their identification papers. The false Arrow Cross men could then use the papers to rescue groups of Jews from their guards.[30]

This Hungarian Jew is dressed in the uniform of the Arrow Cross. Members of the Zionist underground and Wallenberg's staff sometimes used disguises like this to carry out rescue operations.

On one occasion, Wallenberg even considered spreading a rumor that the Swedish houses had been hit by an outbreak of typhus, in order to discourage the Arrow Cross raids. In order to make it convincing, he asked Barna Yaron, a young healthy Jewish man, to agree to be injected with the virus so a doctor could confirm a true case of the disease. "I was young and strong in those days," said Yaron, "so I said 'What the hell' and agreed, but I can tell you I was really scared."[31] He and Wallenberg went to a clinic, but the Jewish doctor became worried that a real epidemic would result and refused to give Yaron the injection.[32]

Perhaps Wallenberg's most useful connection was with Pál Szalai, a Hungarian police officer whose job was to coordinate efforts of the Hungarian police with the Arrow Cross. Szalai did not agree with the philosophy of the Nyilas party, and he decided to use his authority to work against the Arrow Cross from within. Szalai secretly worked against the Szálasi regime by organizing other Hungarian officers like himself who did not support the Nyilas party. Szalai's men sometimes guarded the gates of the ghetto, to be sure that food deliveries got through. When Wallenberg had exhausted other means of rescue, he turned to Szalai for help. His men were often able to rescue Jews who had been taken from the protected houses.

Wallenberg's relationship with Szalai became especially useful on the morning of December 26, when the Arrow Cross still held control of the Swedish legation. Wallenberg arranged for a group of ten Hungarian gendarmes to come to the legation office. They announced to the Arrow Cross guards that they had orders to relieve them. The Arrow Cross left, and the gendarmes turned the legation back to the Swedes and took over guarding the legation against further raids.[33]

Despite Szalai's influence, most of the Arrow Cross was beyond control. They began to roam the streets in gangs, as eager to steal and plunder as they were to kill. Rival Arrow Cross gangs murdered each other over valuables and food. Young Jewish girls were captured and raped. On December 29, forty Arrow Cross troopers invaded the Swiss Glass House and drove fifteen hundred Jews into the streets. That same day they invaded a hospital, killing patients, nurses, and doctors. Karl Müller was arrested and taken to Arrow Cross headquarters, where he saw that one of the Arrow Cross leaders had photos of Wallenberg that he plastered on the walls and gave to all his officers. "If this low-class Jew-lover ever sets foot in Buda, shoot him on the spot," he told them.[34]

Madness and Despair

Despite the chaos in Budapest, the Hungarian government was still operating from its new base in Sopron, issuing new decrees and giving orders. Szálasi himself participated in séances during which he claimed to be in contact with a Scottish ghost who told him that the Allies would soon be defeated.[35] Minister of the Interior Gábor Vajna issued a decree that all streets and public buildings named after Jews must be renamed immediately. Even when the city was completely cut off, the Hungarian and German military leaders promised the troops in Budapest that they would arrange for food, ammunition, and other supplies to be dropped into the city. The Hungarians refused a Soviet offer to accept surrender.

Those in the central ghetto still waited for the arrival of the Soviets. They did not know what to expect but were certain it had to be better than what they were living through. Many gave up hope and committed suicide. Some killed themselves and their children as well. The Institute of Forensic Medicine

103

Ottó Komoly

Ottó Komoly was born in Budapest in 1892. He joined the Hungarian army during World War I, and was honored for his heroism. As Hitler's power began growing in Europe, Komoly became outspoken as a Zionist. He believed that the only way for the Jews to keep their religious and cultural identity without fear of persecution was to form an independent Jewish state in Palestine.[36]

In 1943, Komoly became a leader in the Relief and Rescue Committee of Budapest. The organization worked to save Jews who were being persecuted by the Nazis. Through his work with the secret operation Tiyyul ("Excursion"), he was successful in locating many Polish Jews and bringing them to safety in Hungary.[37] When Germany invaded Hungary, Komoly began helping Jews in his own country. Because of his status as a war hero, he was exempted from the Jewish decrees and could travel freely throughout Budapest. He was assigned the leadership of Section A, and focused his efforts on the rescue of Jewish children. Komoly worked with Wallenberg and Lutz to prevent the children in the Red Cross protected houses from being relocated to the ghetto. Despite their efforts, the children were moved.[38]

On December 31, 1944, Ottó Komoly was abducted by a Nyilas gang and murdered. He was later awarded the Hungarian Order of Freedom.[39]

in Budapest reported that the number of suicides in the month of December 1944 was greater than the total for the whole year of 1943.[40] On New Year's Eve, Ottó Komoly, who had worked tirelessly to serve Jewish children through his work with Red Cross Section A, was dragged from his office in the Ritz Hotel and murdered. Would the new year and the Soviets bring relief for the Jews of Budapest?

9

Liberation and Imprisonment

Despite the troubles and tragedy in Budapest, the year 1945 seemed to offer some hope. It would certainly mean the end of the war and the defeat of the Germans. It would also surely bring the Soviets into Budapest any day to free the Jews from the Arrow Cross.

Wallenberg had big plans for the months ahead. He had been working for months on an elaborate plan that included meeting the immediate needs of food, clothing, and housing for the Jews, as well as helping them locate members of their families who had been taken to concentration camps or labor brigades. He also considered ways of getting them established into business and industry again. He had even created a plan to help them recover their lost property. As soon as the Soviets took Budapest from the Germans, Wallenberg could present his plan to the new government.

At the moment, however, he had more immediate concerns. In the last few days, many Jews and others had lost their lives. After the Glass House of the Swiss legation was invaded, Arthur Weisz, the building's former owner, tried to negotiate with the Arrow Cross. Failing at that, he contacted Pál Szalai, the Hungarian police officer who had helped Wallenberg return Jews to the protected houses. With Szalai's help, eight hundred people were returned to the Glass House. Weisz, however, was not so fortunate. The following day he was captured by the Arrow Cross and never seen again.[1]

Deadly Plans

Interior Minister Gábor Vajna was still in Sopron with the other leaders of the Szálasi government. His cousin, Dr. Ernö Vajna, was now operating as "Representative of the Arrow Cross Party for Defending Budapest." Despite Gábor Vajna's decree in December that all Jews move to the ghetto, thousands were still in hiding or in protected houses. On January 2, Ernö Vajna issued an order that all Jews must move on foot to the main ghetto within three days. Wallenberg immediately sent an official protest to Vajna's office, insisting that this move would result in the starvation of thousands of people, since the ghetto was already not receiving food and the Jews could not leave it to obtain any food for themselves. The addition of thousands more people into the ghetto would mean certain starvation to almost everyone. He pointed out that even jailers have an obligation to feed their prisoners, and called the plan "crazy and inhuman."[2] Wallenberg's protest did not convince Vajna to change his mind. In fact, on January 4, Vajna increased his demand by giving the Jews just one hour to complete their move to the main ghetto. The next day, five thousand Jews were marched from the protected houses to the fenced main ghetto.[3]

In a desperate move to save the rest, Wallenberg offered Vajna a deal on January 6. Wallenberg knew that the Jews were

107

not the only hungry people in the city of Budapest. Because of the Soviet blockade around the city, Hungarian citizens and soldiers were also running out of food. In exchange for allowing the Jews in protected houses to stay there and keeping a hospital open in the international ghetto, Wallenberg agreed to hand over food from his stockpile to the Hungarian government.

The Loyal Szalai

Like Wallenberg, Pál Szalai recognized the danger to those still living in the international ghetto. Szalai used his influence in the Hungarian police force to arrange for a guard unit of one hundred policemen to protect the ghetto from Arrow Cross attack. He ordered his men to protect the ghetto from all forced entry, even if it required killing the intruders. Szalai also offered two bodyguards to protect Wallenberg, as he had heard of more threats against the diplomat's life. Wallenberg, however, refused the offer. "I'm not going to take any more care of my person than I do of my signatures," he told Szalai.[4] By this time, Wallenberg was signing passes for anyone who asked. Each one represented a chance for someone to survive.

Szalai's guard could not provide enough protection to stop the violence, and not all of them were loyal. On January 8, the Arrow Cross invaded the Swedish legation offices on both Jokai Street and Üllöi Street. At the Üllöi office, the residents were marched out of the building past Szalai's guard, who merely watched as they were taken. The victims were taken to an Arrow Cross building for interrogation. There they were ordered to hand over their coats, shoes, and any other valuables they might have on them. A few were beaten before Szalai's loyal guard came to their rescue. They were finally returned to the Üllöi office.

Those from the Jokai office were not so fortunate. Two hundred eighty Jews, both adults and children, were taken to an Arrow Cross cellar. Over the next few days groups were forced to perform labor around Budapest. At the end of each day, that day's group was taken to the bank of the Danube where they were executed. Some escaped or bribed their guards, but one hundred eighty of the Jews from the Jokai Street office were killed.[5]

During the second week of January, Szalai again proved his loyalty to Wallenberg and his rescue effort. Szalai's contacts within the police department discovered that hundreds of German and Arrow Cross officers were gathering in the ghetto, planning to destroy the remaining Jews before the Soviets took the city. The Arrow Cross intended to use machine guns to wipe out all Jews within the fence. Szalai went to see Ernö Vajna and sent an officer to tell Wallenberg what was happening. Vajna would do nothing to stop the attack. Wallenberg knew it was too dangerous to go in person, but he sent Szalai to tell German General August Schmidthuber to call off the attack, or else face war trials on a charge of mass murder. Schmidthuber, unwilling to place his own life at risk, ordered the plan stopped at the last moment.[6]

A Hunted Man

On January 10, the members of the Swedish legation decided it was too dangerous to remain in Pest. Anger pleaded with Wallenberg to move with the others to the other side of the river, as Buda seemed safer at the moment, but Wallenberg decided to stay in Pest with those he wanted to protect. He intended to make the first contact with the Soviets on behalf of the Jews.

He spent a night in the vault of the Hazai Bank, along with his photographer, Tom Veres, his driver, Vilmos Langfelder, and several Jewish families. When Szalai stopped in for a visit, Wallenberg was pleased to show him their temporary shelter. "Did you ever see a bank vault anywhere in the world which held greater treasure than this one?" he asked his friend. "Human lives are much greater than silver or gold."[7]

Langfelder drove Wallenberg and Veres up Gellért Hill to the Citadel, the highest hill in the area, to see how the war was going. Along the road, the smell of unburied and decomposing bodies was almost overwhelming. From the top of the hill they could see the smoking ruins of the once-magnificent hotels and concert halls of the city. The bridges across the Danube were still intact, for the time being. The men could see the flashes of artillery as the German and Soviet troops fired at each other. Although the Germans were still fighting, it was clear that the Soviets were advancing on them. It would be over soon.[8]

During the night of January 11, Wallenberg went to the Red Cross headquarters on Benczur Street. Because of its location, it seemed likely that this part of Pest would be the first to be taken by the Soviets. Wallenberg hoped that would give him the opportunity to introduce himself to the Soviet officials and present his plan for rehabilitation of the Jews. Now there was little for him to do except wait.

On January 12, he made a last trip to the Üllöi office. There he found many more requests for protective passes. Although

Thomas Veres was a Hungarian Jewish photographer. During the final months of the German occupation of Budapest, he served as the official photographer of Raoul Wallenberg.

he felt there was little need for them now, he signed them all. There was no point in refusing any request at this point. He stopped by the legation office on Vadász Street to pick up papers and money he had left there for safekeeping.

The Soviets Arrive

Wallenberg had not been able to see from the hilltop that the Soviets had discovered the underground network of cellars that connected many of the buildings in Pest. On January 13, a thump came from behind the cellar wall of the cellar of the Red Cross headquarters on Benczur Street. After a few minutes, twenty Soviet soldiers emerged through a hole in the wall. Wallenberg presented both the German and Soviet versions of his diplomatic papers and asked to meet with an officer in charge. Within a short time several officers arrived. Wallenberg left with the Soviets to go to their headquarters.[9]

Although accounts of Wallenberg's experiences in the three days following his unexpected first meeting with the Soviets differ, it is likely that he was questioned by several different Soviet officials, including the Soviet secret police (the NKVD) in several different sessions. Wallenberg had studied Russian in high school because he thought it would be a useful language in the future.[10] Still, he spoke German far better than he spoke Russian. A secretary who was present during one of the interrogation sessions believed that the Soviets thought Wallenberg was a German spy.[11]

For the next several days, the Soviets continued to advance through Pest, liberating more areas from German control. Wallenberg traveled around within the liberated areas, making preparations to present himself to the Soviets in Debrecen to begin his work for the post-war Jewish community. Vilmos Langfelder drove Wallenberg in the legation car, but they were continually accompanied by Soviet guards. Wallenberg went to visit several of the legation offices to gather a few belongings and to pick up some cash he had left there. He decided to leave most of the money, so it could to be used to buy food and protection for Jews.

"My Work Has not Been in Vain"

On January 16, the Soviets liberated the international ghetto. On the morning of January 17, the main ghetto was liberated. The liberation was not without more bloodshed for the Jews, however. In the final moments of battle, Nazi and Arrow Cross soldiers tried to protect themselves from Soviet fire by using Jews as human shields. In all, three thousand of the ghetto's inhabitants lost their lives in the final hours of fighting before the liberation.[12]

Still, many survived. Twenty-five thousand people in the international ghetto and sixty-nine thousand in the main ghetto had survived the German occupation of Hungary, many because of the efforts of Raoul Wallenberg.[13] At one of his last stops before leaving the city, Wallenberg observed three Jewish men, still wearing their yellow stars on their coats, coming out of a nearby house into the street for the first time in weeks. He turned to his friend Pál Nevi, "So you see, I *have* succeeded; my work has not been in vain."[14]

Langfelder was at the wheel of Wallenberg's car as they prepared to leave Budapest on January 17. A longtime friend of Wallenberg, László Petö, accompanied them. Three Soviet soldiers escorted them: two on a motorcycle, one in an attached sidecar. Wallenberg was going to Debrecen, 120 miles east of Budapest. There he hoped to meet with Marshal Rodion Malinovsky, a commanding officer of the Soviet army. Wallenberg gathered his knapsack, a sleeping bag, a few clothes, and some money. He told his friends that he expected to be back in about a week.

According to Petö, Wallenberg was in high spirits and eagerly anticipating his meeting with Malinovsky. He had no reason to think that the Soviets might not share his enthusiasm for helping Jews. The Soviets were, after all, the liberators. He pointed to the Soviet escorts and joked, "I don't know whether I'm going as a prisoner or as a guest."[15] Shortly after the trip began, the car had a minor collision with a Soviet truck. Angry Soviet soldiers jumped out of the truck and began threatening Langfelder, but the escorting Soviet officers managed to calm them down by informing them that a diplomat was in the car. Before they reached the edge of town, Petö changed his mind about making the trip and got out of the car. He watched while the car with Wallenberg and Langfelder disappeared. It was the last time their friends would ever see them.

Soviet "Liberation"

In the days that followed, few people noticed that Wallenberg had not returned. By January 18, Pest was freed of Nazi control, and the Soviets marched on. As the Soviets completed the liberation of Pest, the Germans and Hungarians withdrew across the Danube into Buda, blowing up the bridges behind them. The newly-liberated Jews of Pest tore down the fence around the main ghetto. Their relief at their liberation did not last long, however. Although their Nazi oppressors were gone, they now faced a new set of invaders: thousands of hungry Soviet soldiers who cared little about the Jews' troubles.

Instead of giving aid and comfort to the Jews, the soldiers went from house to house through the city looking for food, liquor, and any valuables they could find. They considered non-Jewish Hungarians to be German sympathizers and blamed them for delaying the war's end. Women of all ages were victims of rape. After escaping an Arrow Cross roundup, Kate Lebovitz's Swedish pass allowed her to wait out the "liberation" in a protected house in the international ghetto. For her and many others, Soviet occupation was no improvement over the Arrow Cross regime. "It was the same except for the uniforms," Kate said. "First green uniforms, then red, but it was the same."[16]

In Buda, the Arrow Cross terror continued. Nyilas troops attacked two Jewish hospitals, executing doctors, nurses, and patients. Per Anger and the remaining members of the Swedish legation took refuge in the legation building in the Castle Hill district. They did not yet know of Wallenberg's disappearance. They had their own problems to deal with. Soviet soldiers were already on the Buda side of the river before the Nazis had destroyed the bridges over the Danube. Troops fought street to street. Each morning, Soviet planes flew over Buda, strafing the streets with machine-gun fire. Artillery in Pest continually bombarded Buda with shells. There was no electricity, gas, or running water. Telephones worked sometimes. Food supplies were nearly nonexistent. When a horse was killed by gunfire in the street near the legation, dozens of people rushed out of nearby buildings to cut meat from it. Its carcass was stripped clean in a matter of minutes. Anger and the other Swedes prepared horse goulash and were grateful that it lasted several days.[17]

Near the end of January, Anger and another Swede left Castle Hill to see if conditions were any better at the legation building in the Rose Hill district. After a perilous journey that included dodging gunfire, they arrived at Rose Hill to find it also damaged by artillery shells, but still habitable. They decided to stay there because it was nearer the war's front. They hoped, as had Wallenberg, that early contact with the Soviets would gain protection for them and their property as diplomats. When the Soviets arrived on January 30, the officers were only slightly impressed by their diplomatic credentials, but more impressed by their Swiss watches. They demanded the watches at gunpoint, then took up residence in the house, where they helped themselves to the food and wine there. The only advantage was that they placed guards at the house for the month the diplomats remained there, thus protecting them from being looted by other Soviet troops in the area.[18]

Invasion of the Legation

Back at the Castle Hill office, the Soviets invaded the legation and broke into the files and safes. They questioned the staff. Wallenberg's files were taken. Lars Berg was arrested in Pest and interrogated about Wallenberg's work and the legation's activities in Budapest. Later, Berg reported that the NKVD believed that Wallenberg's and Berg's humanitarian mission was a cover, and the men were actually high-level Nazi spies. Berg was finally released. Many Red Cross workers were questioned about their work in Budapest and accused of espionage. George Wilhelm of Red Cross Section B was held for several months in a Soviet prison. On April 18, Anger and the rest of the Swedish diplomatic corps returned home to Stockholm, after stopovers in Moscow and Bucharest, Romania. They still did not know Wallenberg was missing.

Missing Diplomat

Few facts are known about Wallenberg's fate after January 17, 1945. Soviet Vice Commissar of Foreign Affairs Vladamir Dekanusov sent a message to Staffan Söderblom, Swedish ambassador in Moscow, on January 17, that Wallenberg had been found. It reported that Wallenberg was under the protection of Soviet military authorities.[19] Two weeks later, Wallenberg's mother, Maj von Dardel, met with the Soviet ambassador in Stockholm, Madame Alexandra Kollontai. Kollontai assured Maj that her son was safe and would soon come home. It was the only reassuring news about her son that she would ever receive. On March 8, 1945, the Soviet controlled radio service in Budapest announced that Wallenberg had been murdered in Budapest by German Gestapo officers. His friends did not believe it.

Only Wallenberg could tell the truth of all that happened to him after January 17, but his voice has never been heard. Instead, a story must be pieced together on the basis of testimony of those who claim to have seen and communicated with him during the years that followed. The fate of Vilmos Langfelder is also a mystery. It appears that perhaps Wallenberg and Langfelder were victims of an international political situation they could never have anticipated: the Cold War.

As soon as the Germans were defeated, an alliance fell apart. The Soviet Union no longer held good relations with the United States, Great Britain, or other nations with whom she had been allied during the long fight against Hitler. The Swedish government, although still neutral, was clearly afraid of the power demonstrated by the Soviets. Per Anger noted that, as the Swedish diplomats were returning to their homeland, Minster Söderblom took him aside and told him, "Remember, when you get home to Sweden—not one harsh word about the Russians!"[20] This attitude would play an important role in Wallenberg's and Langfelder's fate.

Söderblom's Indifference

Over the next few months and years, little real information about Wallenberg was available. On March 8, Söderblom was ordered by the Swedish Foreign Office to ask the Soviets for an investigation into the whereabouts of Wallenberg, but he did not. Instead, he sent that order to Patrik Reuterswärd, the Swedish minister in Bucharest.[21] In April, Valdemar Langlet of the Swedish Red Cross wrote a letter stating his theory that Wallenberg had been murdered by the Arrow Cross.[22]

Söderblom seemed to accept this theory, especially since it made his situation easier. He had experienced problems dealing with the Soviets on matters related to Swedish business in Soviet territories. According to a 2003 Swedish report, he "wanted to remove [the Wallenberg case] from the agenda of his legation."[23] Reuterswärd also sent incomplete information to the Swedish Foreign Ministry. He did not tell them of eyewitness reports that Wallenberg had been taken prisoner by the Soviets. Reuterswärd may have withheld this information because he knew his reports were being intercepted and censored by the Soviets. Even so, he did not file the reports later when it would have been possible to send them safely.[24]

Although it appeared that Söderblom and Reuterswärd wanted to forget about Wallenberg, other people did not. Rudolph Philipp, an Austrian journalist who had fled the Nazi takeover of his own country, began investigating the Wallenberg case. In November 1946, he published a book based on his own research and the testimony of former Soviet prisoners who claimed that Wallenberg was alive.

In December 1945, Söderblom again attempted to close the Wallenberg case. A letter from Söderblom that month stated that he believed Wallenberg was dead. On December 26, he wrote to Aleksander Abramov of the Soviet Commisariat of Foreign Affairs that "it would be splendid if the legation were to be given a reply in this spirit, that is to say, that Wallenberg is dead."[25] The following spring, however, in talks with Abramov, Söderblom heard hints that perhaps Wallenberg was not dead. Söderblom sent a letter to Swedish Foreign Minister Östen Undén that Wallenberg "might after all be alive and identified in some camp or so."[26] Neither of them shared this information with Swedish authorities. Soderblom arranged a meeting with Soviet leader Josef Stalin in June 1946. Unwilling to accuse the Soviets of holding Wallenberg, Söderblom told Stalin he believed Wallenberg had probably been killed in Budapest, but he asked him to see if he could find out any information. Three months later, a message from Stalin informed the Swedish government that it would accept no more inquiries about Wallenberg.

A year later, in 1947, the Soviets released an official report to Söderblom, announcing, "As a result of a careful investigation it has been established that Wallenberg is not in the Soviet Union, and that he is unknown to us."[27] The report indicated that the original message that Wallenberg was in protective custody was incorrect, and that Wallenberg had probably been killed by the Arrow Cross in Budapest. It assured the Swedes that he was not being held in any prison camp.

In 1948, a sculptor created a statue depicting Saint George battling a serpent. The base of the statue had a profile likeness of Wallenberg and the inscription, "This memorial is our silent and eternal gratitude to him and should always remind us of his enduring humanity in a period of inhumanity."[28] The statue was set in Saint Stephen's Park in Budapest. On the morning of the unveiling, the crowd stared at an empty space. During the night, Soviet soldiers had taken the statue away.

Anger on the Case

That year, 1948, Per Anger was reassigned to the Swedish Foreign Office and placed in charge of the Wallenberg case. In his work on the case, Anger made contact with a Swedish journalist, Edward af Sandeberg, who had been arrested in Germany and imprisoned by the Soviets until 1946. Before his imprisonment, af Sandeberg had never heard of Wallenberg. In prison, a German inmate who claimed to have shared a cell with Wallenberg in Lefortovo prison told af Sandeberg his story. Anger also read the evidence Rudolph Philipp had collected. He learned that five Swiss diplomats in Budapest had been captured by the Soviets and taken to prison. A year later, the Swiss offered to exchange several Soviet prisoners for the Swiss diplomats. The Soviets accepted the offer and returned the Swiss citizens.

By 1950, Anger was convinced that Wallenberg was alive in a Soviet prison. He suggested to Östen Undén, Swedish foreign minister, that a similar trade of several Soviet prisoners might be offered for Wallenberg's return. Undén refused to consider it. "The Swedish government does not do such things," he told Anger.[29] Anger was convinced that the Swedish government was not willing to take action. He asked to be removed from the Wallenberg case.

Why did the Swedish government hesitate to investigate further? According to a 2003 report of the Swedish Ministry of Foreign Affairs, Söderblom and Undén were largely to blame, along with Swedish Foreign Minister Christian Günther and Ulf Barck-Holst of the Swedish legation. If they had taken seriously and released the information that suggested that Wallenberg could be alive, it "could have led the Swedish side to take a different course of action."[30]

Eyewitness Accounts

In 1951, a group of political prisoners was freed by the Soviet government. Among them was an Italian named Claudio de Mohr, who had been captured and imprisoned in 1944. He reported that the prisoners in Lefortovo were not allowed to talk to each other, so they had devised a communication code with which they sent messages by tapping on pipes. According to de Mohr, he had been in a cell next to a German named Willi Roedl and a Swedish diplomat named Raoul Wallenberg. The Italian did not understand why a Swede would be held by the Soviets and asked several times for the message to be repeated. De Mohr reported that his communication with Wallenberg continued for at least two years. Although the Swedish government now pressed the USSR for more information about Wallenberg, Soviet officials continued to deny that they were holding him. Still, de Mohr's account would be just the first of many testimonies that Wallenberg had survived past 1945.

In 1955, more prisoners were freed by the Soviets, and again more stories of Wallenberg's and Langfelder's imprisonment surfaced. The Swedish Foreign Office now began interviewing the released prisoners and recording their testimonies. Each was interviewed separately and was not informed of any testimony given by other prisoners. Only those who had direct contact with Wallenberg or Langfelder were included; no third-party testimony was accepted. Based on the accounts told by these prison survivors, Wallenberg made great efforts to be sure that other prisoners knew his name and country, so that they could tell his government how to find him. The Soviets made even greater efforts to keep Wallenberg's identity and location a secret.

Ottó Scheur and Gustav Richter worked for Hitler before being sent to Lubyanka prison in Moscow. Lubyanka was a temporary holding facility where prisoners were held before being sent to other prisons within the Soviet prison system. Wallenberg was brought to their cell shortly after his arrival at Lubyanka. He told Scheur and Richter about his trip from

121

Budapest and described how the car had been stopped just outside the city, the tires slashed, and guards from the NKVD had taken them to Moscow. Wallenberg told them he believed his predicament was the result of a mistake, and he would be freed any day. Two months later, however, he was taken to Lefortovo prison.

At Lefortovo, Wallenberg shared a cell with Jan Loyda and Wilhelm Roedel, both former Nazis. Loyda had previously shared a cell with Vilmos Langfelder. Wallenberg was pleased that his friend was nearby and asked the guards to give his ration of cigarettes to Langfelder. In the summer of 1946, at about the same time Söderblom met with Stalin, Wallenberg was interrogated at Lefortovo. He told his cell mates that they were accusing him of being a spy for the Americans and the British. The interrogators also told him his government did not want him back.

The following summer, 1947, ten prisoners were separately interrogated about their knowledge of Wallenberg and whom they had told about him. Afterward, they were all kept in solitary confinement. One of them, Horst Kistchmann asked why and was told he was sent to solitary "as punishment for having told your cell-mates about Langfelder and Wallenberg."[31] At about this time, Wallenberg was apparently moved to another prison. This was also when the Soviets released the report that they had never held Wallenberg in custody and knew nothing of him.

Dead in 1947?

The testimonies gathered after 1955 gave the Swedish government cause to again ask for more information from the Soviets. In 1957, they did respond, but this time with a very different answer: Wallenberg was dead. They reported that he had been held in secret and had died of a heart attack on July 16,

1947, in Lubyanka prison. The report also indicated that the Secret Police officer responsible for holding Wallenberg, Viktor Abakumov, had lied to the government about it. Moreover, Abakumov had ordered the body cremated without autopsy. Abakumov had been executed in 1954. The memo was signed by Deputy Foreign Minister Andrei Gromyko, who offered his "sincere regrets for what has happened," and his "deep sympathy" to the government and to Wallenberg's family.[32] The report included no reference to Langfelder.

Although this was a severe blow, it was not the end of the story. In 1958, André Shimkevich was pardoned and released from a Soviet prison. He contacted Wallenberg's mother, Maj von Dardel and told her that in December 1947, he shared a cell with her son, but they were not allowed to speak. Shimkevich testified that they communicated through sign language and shared their stories.

In 1961, Dr. Nanna Svartz, who worked as personal physician to Maj von Dardel, attended a medical conference in Moscow. There she engaged Dr. Alexander Myasnikov, a longtime acquaintance, in conversation. She asked him about Wallenberg and he told her that the Swede was in ill health and confined to a mental hospital. Svartz pleaded with Myasnikov for his return. Later, Myasnikov denied the conversation and insisted he had never heard of Wallenberg.

In the years since, several more released prisoners have added clues to the mystery. In the mid-1960s, Soviet General Gennadi Kuprianov was freed from Vladimir prison. He spoke to a few friends about the Swede named Wallenberg whom he had met in Vladimir in 1953, then had seen again in 1955 and 1956. In 1979, he was summoned by the KGB (the same secret police agency that had been known as the NKVD). The Swedish press had heard the story and published it. He was warned not to speak about his time in prison, nor about anyone whom he had met there. Kuprianov was ordered to submit a written denial, but he refused. He did not return home that day, and five days later, he reportedly died of a heart attack at the KGB headquarters.[33]

The Mystery Continues

Even as late as 1978, former prisoners carried stories of an "old Swede" in a psychiatric hospital in Russia, but Soviet officials still insisted that Wallenberg died in 1947. In 1989, the Soviets produced Wallenberg's passport, a permit to carry a gun, and some money. These items had been taken from Wallenberg at the time of his arrest and had reportedly been in an unmarked envelope that was recently discovered by a worker. An article in *U.S. News and World Report* from 1996 includes accounts from several people, including a prison cleaning woman, who say they remember Wallenberg from prison at times after 1947.[34]

In July 2000, a report from Stockholm indicated that Soviet authorities had admitted that Wallenberg probably did not die of natural causes, but was either murdered or executed in Lubyanka. Soviet records declared Wallenberg's case closed in 1947, but a Swedish diplomat suggested that the term "closed" might indicate death or that a prisoner was "allowed to survive with a changed identity."[35] A report from Moscow in December 2000 cited a Soviet report that admitted that Wallenberg and Langfelder were arrested by Soviet authorities and held for over two years. One authority involved in the investigation told an interviewer that a former KGB chief had told him Wallenberg was executed.[36]

Although Wallenberg's fate may never be clear, his impact on the lives of thousands stands as testament to the extraordinary power of one individual.

10

Rescuer or Spy?

When the Soviets first took Wallenberg into custody, they may have believed he was a spy for the Nazis. According to the testimony of his gulag cell mates, they soon became convinced he was a spy for the Americans or the British. A letter dated June 15, 1945, from War Refugee Board (WRB) representative Iver Olsen to the director of the WRB in Washington, D.C., stated, "We are informed that [Wallenberg] kept extremely complete and documented records of a highly interesting nature, and that these records were still in the Swedish legation when the staff was forced to leave Budapest."[1] If Soviet agents seized these files from the Swedish legation office, they certainly would have found records of money received from the WRB and the Jewish Joint Distribution Committee in America.

Anti-Semitism among the Soviet government also played a role. Those who interrogated Wallenberg often questioned his motives, as they could see no logical reason why a Swedish

Gentile would risk his life for Jews. After one interrogation, he told his cell mates the Soviets had asked him, "Why would a rich Swede, a capitalist, a Christian, undertake that kind of work? Come on. You are a spy."[2] In fact, his family ties may have made his situation more difficult, since some industries owned by the Wallenberg family supplied ball bearings and steel to the German war effort.[3]

Wallenberg an OSS Operative?

In the mid-1990s, the Central Intelligence Agency (CIA) declassified a number of documents from the 1940s. Among them were documents related to the WRB and its connection to the Office of Strategic Services (OSS), America's earlier version of the CIA. The papers suggest that Olsen worked for both the WRB and the OSS in Stockholm. Photographer Tom Veres took hundreds of pictures of German actions against Jews and of Wallenberg's rescue activities. He also took photos of Soviet military positions on that January night when he went with Wallenberg and Langfelder to the top of Castle Hill. Veres' film was regularly sent with the diplomatic pouch to Stockholm; was it used by American intelligence agencies? A list of people who worked for the OSS during that period does include Wallenberg, but a former OSS officer insists that "Wallenberg was not on the OSS payroll."[4] Because Wallenberg used WRB funds for rescue efforts and did not receive a salary from the OSS, it would be difficult to call him an OSS agent. Still, if the Soviets knew of Olsen's connection to the OSS and discovered Wallenberg's letters to him detailing the use of WRB funds, it would make them suspect that Wallenberg was a spy.

Despite the records contained in these documents, Wallenberg's service to mankind remains unquestionable. Lars Berg, who worked side by side with Wallenberg, has said,

"One who had seen Raoul work the clock around, week after week, knew that Wallenberg had not had a moment free for spying."[5] Clearly, Wallenberg considered his own mission that of saving lives.

Wallenberg's Impact

According to the statistical department of the World Jewish Congress, 762,007 Jews were living in Hungary at the time of the German occupation in March 1944. At the end of the war, 255,500 Hungarian Jews (about one third of the original number) had survived. This total includes those who were liberated from concentration camps, those who returned from labor service, as well as those who survived long enough to be liberated in Budapest.[6] The largest numbers of Jews were lost from the provinces during the months of May through July when Eichmann organized the massive transports to the gas chambers of Auschwitz. Olsen admits, ". . . the only regrettable thing is that the War Refugee Board was not established a year or two earlier."[7]

There is no doubt that Eichmann planned to annihilate the entire Jewish population of Hungary. Why did the neutral nations wait nearly six months after the German occupation to step in to help the Jews? According to historian Yehuda Bauer, they wanted to be on good terms with the Allies when it became clear that the Germans would soon be defeated. "The war was nearing its end and the neutrals were increasingly motivated to take a stand against the losing Germans. The protection of Jews was a relatively easy way of showing identification with the Allied war aims."[8]

How effective was Wallenberg? One hundred nineteen thousand Jews were liberated in Budapest.[9] This was the single largest Jewish community to survive in any Nazi-controlled country in Europe. Between fifteen thousand and twenty thousand of them had Swedish papers.[10] No one knows how many more of the survivors were saved through Wallenberg's efforts to distribute food and medicine to those in the international ghetto, as well as to those in hiding and others in the main ghetto. Additionally, Wallenberg's effective bribery of Arrow Cross soldiers and Nazi officials and his connections with the Hungarian gendarmes through Pál Szalai saved hundreds from deportation, the death marches, and the threatened annihilation of the main ghetto in the final days of the war. A letter from Iver Olsen to the WRB in June 1945 estimated that the "Hungarian rescue and relief actions initiated by the War Refugee Board from Sweden . . . paved the way for saving the lives of perhaps 100,000 Jews."[11]

But Wallenberg could not have saved so many without the help of many others who shared his mission. Lars Berg, Per Anger, and Ivan Danielsson of the Swedish legation had already established the distribution of Schutz-passes before Wallenberg's arrival. They continued to work with Wallenberg and joined him on missions to save protected Jews from deportation and the death marches.

The Red Cross was also vital to the success of the rescue work in Budapest. Valdemar Langlet, Friedrich Born, George

Wallenberg saved thousands of Jews from the fate of the concentration camps. These emaciated Hungarian Jewish survivors pose in a barracks in the newly liberated Ampfing concentration camp, a sub-camp of the main camp in Dachau. Dachau was located in Germany.

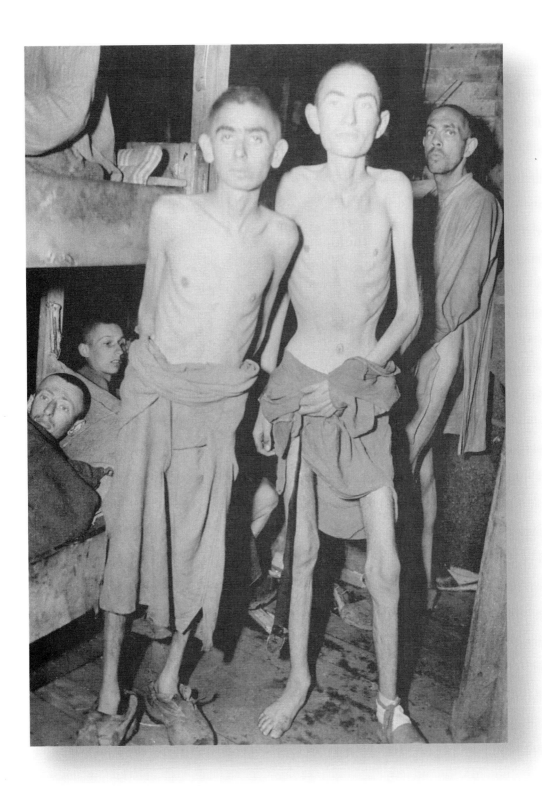

Wilhelm, and Ottó Komoly all worked tirelessly to provide food, clothing, medical care, and safe houses for Jews, especially children. The Red Cross, under Born's direction, is credited with saving between eleven thousand and fifteen thousand people.

Other foreign diplomats like Carl Lutz of Switzerland, Giorgio Perlasca and Angel Sanz-Briz of Spain, and Monsignor Angelo Rotta who represented the Catholic Church as papal nuncio, provided passes and baptismal papers to Hungarian Jews and operated protected houses. Lutz's operation issued over sixty-two thousand passes. The Spanish legation issued nearly four thousand, and Rotta's work resulted in certificates for fifteen thousand Jews and hundreds more were saved through protection provided by monasteries.[12]

Individuals who chose to defy the Nazi government and provide aid to the Jews made a difference. Some were people of influence such as Baroness Elizabeth Kemény and Pál Szalai. Others were friends and neighbors who hid Jewish citizens and provided food. Still others were the courageous members of the Jewish underground who participated in daring schemes to rescue and provide aid to their fellow Jews.

All these people and organizations played important roles in saving the Jewish population of Budapest, and all acknowledge that Wallenberg's courage and untiring dedication to the rescue work inspired them to keep working despite the overwhelming odds against their success.

In 1948, Albert Einstein nominated Wallenberg for the Nobel Peace Prize. In 1981, President Ronald Reagan pronounced Wallenberg an honorary United States citizen. Today, Yad Vashem, the Holocaust Martyrs' and Heroes' Remembrance Authority, recognizes the contributions of

Kate Stern was born in 1926 in Budapest. When the Germans occupied Hungary, Kate's family moved to the Jewish ghetto. At eighteen, Kate married Eugene Lebovitz, a Jew from Czechoslovakia. They began working for the Jewish youth resistance group Halutzim and cooperating with Wallenberg's rescue work. Wallenberg made a strong impression on Kate. "He was a very nice man, very handsome, very distinguished, very powerful. You looked at him and trusted him."[13]

Late one night, Kate's family was awakened by Arrow Cross guards. "They said it was an air raid and we had to go to a synagogue. There they shined a light into our faces. 'You go here. [to the door on the left] You go here [to the right]'"[14] Kate, her mother, and Eugene were led through the door on the right. Her father and brothers were taken through the door on the left. Her father was taken to the Danube River and shot. Her brothers died in concentration camps.

Eugene was taken to Mauthausen camp, but Kate got a protective pass from Wallenberg. She believes she would not be alive if not for his help. "He was a living hero," she says. "He shows that one person can make a big difference."[15]

Kate and Eugene were reunited after the war, and they emigrated to New York. In the 1960s, they moved to Kansas, where they live today. The author interviewed the Lebovitzes for this book.

those who dared to rescue others at the risk of their own lives and careers. As of January 1, 2004, Yad Vashem had honored nearly 20,205 people from 40 different countries as "Righteous Among the Nations."[16] Among them are many who worked with Wallenberg, such as Anger, Berg, Langlet, Danielsson, Lutz, Perlasca, and Born. Wallenberg was honored by Yad Vashem in 1966.[17]

Wallenberg's Legacy

After the war, Eugene Lebovitz was liberated from Mauthausen concentration camp and made his way back to Budapest to find Kate. With the Soviet occupation, they did not wish to remain in Hungary, especially considering the fact that Kate was pregnant with their child. The Lebovitzes walked from Budapest to the Austrian border, traveling at night to avoid being stopped by the Soviets. Once in Austria, they made contact with the underground Palestine Brigade who transported them by truck to a displaced persons camp in Italy. They tried to travel to Palestine but were worried that their ship would be turned away by the British and forced to go to Cypress instead. Finally, they traveled to New York where they could stay with relatives temporarily. Eugene, whose father had been a tailor, soon found work with a pattern maker in New York, and the young family began a new life.[18]

Today, Kate and Eugene Lebovitz live in a quiet suburban neighborhood in Kansas. Their four children earned college degrees and have successful careers. Their grandchildren's and great-grandchildren's photos decorate their home. Eugene sometimes visits schools with his son, Allen, to talk about the Holocaust. It is not so easy for Kate. Her memories of those frightful days in Hungary haunt her. She is reluctant to speak of her experiences, and even reading books about the

Holocaust is difficult for her. Allen Lebovitz is quick to acknowledge that, "Without Wallenberg, my family would not exist. It is an important story that needs to be told."[19] The Lebovitzes and hundreds of thousands of others are living proof that Wallenberg's desire, "to save a nation," has been fulfilled.

TIMELINE

Shaded areas indicate events in the life of Raoul Wallenberg

1912

August: Raoul Gustav Wallenberg born.

1931

Wallenberg begins studying architecture at University of Michigan.

1933

Hitler becomes chancellor of Germany

March 22: Concentration camp at Dachau opens.

April 26: Gestapo established

May 10: Nazis burn banned books in public

1934

August 2: Hitler names himself "Fuhrer," or leader, of Germany

1935

Wallenberg graduates; begins work in Cape Town, South Africa.

May 31: Jews in Germany no longer allowed to serve in armed forces.

September 15: Anti-Jewish Nuremberg Laws are enacted; Jews are no longer considered citizens of Germany.

1936

Wallenberg begins work in Haifa, Palestine; learns of German Holocaust.

Nazis boycott Jewish-owned businesses.

March 7: Nazis occupy Rhineland.

July: Sachsenhausen concentration camp opened.

July: Wallenberg returns to Sweden for military service.

1937

July 15: Buchenwald concentration camp opens.

1937–1941
Wallenberg has several failed business ventures in Europe.

1938
March: Mauthausen concentration camp opens.

March 13: Germany annexs Austria and applies all anti-Jewish laws there.

July 6: League of Nations holds conference on Jewish refugees at Evian, France, but no action is taken to help the refugees.

October 5: All Jewish passports must now be stamped with a red "J."

October 15: Nazi troops occupy the Sudentenland.

November 9-10: Kirstallnacht, the Night of the Broken Glass; Jewish businesses and synagogues are destroyed and thirty thousand Jews are sent to concentration camps.

1939
March 15: Germans occupy Czechoslovakia.

August 23: Germany and the Soviet Union sign a non-agression pact.

September 1: Germany invades Poland, beginning World War II.

October 28: First Polish ghetto established in Piotrkow.

November 23: Jews in Poland are forced to wear an arm band or yellow star.

1940
April 9: Germans occupy Denmark and southern Norway.

May 7: Lodz Ghetto is established,

May 20: Auschwitz concentration camp is established.

June 22: France surrenders to Germany.

September 27: Germany, Italy and Japan form the Axis powers.

November 16: Warsaw Ghetto is established.

1941

June 22: Germany invades the Soviet Union.

October: Auschwitz II (Birkenau) death camp is established.

1942

January 20: Wannsee Conference in Berlin where the "Final Solution" is outlined.

March 17: Killings begin at Belzec death camp.

May: Killings begin at Sobibor death camp.

July22: Treblinka concentration camp is established.

Summer-Winter: Mass deportations to death camps begin.

1943

March: Liquidation of Krakow Ghetto begins.

April 19: Warsaw ghetto uprising.

Fall: Liquidation of Minsk, Vilna, and Riga ghettos.

1942–1944

Wallenberg works for Koloman Lauer; travels throughout Nazi-occupied Europe.

1944

March 19: Germans invade and occupy Hungary; Eichmann arrives.

May 15: Jewish deportations from Hungary begin, most sent to Auschwitz.

June 23: Wallenberg hired by War Refugee Board and Swedish Foreign Office.

June 24: Budapest Jews moved to yellow-star houses.

July 8: Horthy stops deportations; 476,000 Jews already gone.

July 9: Wallenberg arrives in Budapest.

July 14: Soviet forces liberate Majdanek death camp.

July 17: Wallenberg sends first report; already has begun work on Schutz-passes.

August 12: Wallenberg meets with Horthy; Horthy agrees to honor Swedish passes.

Mid-August: Ferenczy allows Wallenberg to set up special houses for "Swedish" Jews.

August 24: Horthy stops Eichmann's plan to deport Budapest Jews; Eichmann leaves.

August 25: Horthy fires pro-Nazi Prime Minister Sztójay; appoints Géza Lakatos.

September 12: Wallenberg's letter to Stockholm tells of frequent air raids; suggests war may be over soon.

October 11: Horthy agrees to surrender to the Soviets.

October 15: Horthy announces that Hungary is now allied with Russia; Horthy's son kidnapped; Horthy overthrown by Szálasi's Nyilas party.

October 20: Jewish draft for labor brigades begins.

November 2: Soviets break through defenses near Budapest; Jews in labor brigades massacred by Hungarian soldiers

November 7: Szálasi orders protected Jews into confined international ghetto.

November 8: Death marches to Hegyeshalom begin.

December 8: Soviet siege of Budapest begins.

December 22: Eichmann attempts to assassinate Jewish Council; leaves Budapest.

December 24: Increased terrorism against Jews begins, including raids of legation offices, protected houses, children's homes, and hospitals.

1945

January 2: Ernö Vajna orders all protected Jews to move to main ghetto; Wallenberg protests.

January 6: Wallenberg strikes deal with Vajna to give food to Hungarians in exchange for allowing protected Jews to stay in international ghetto.

January 10: Swedish legation moves from Pest to Buda; Wallenberg remains alone.

January 13: Soviet troops enter Benczur Street Red Cross building; capture Wallenberg.

January 16: International ghetto is liberated by Soviet troops.

January 17: Main ghetto liberated; Wallenberg and Vilmos Langfelder leave Budapest with Soviet military escort; they are never seen again.

Auschwitz inmates begin death march.

April 6–10: Buchenwald inmates sent on death march.

April 30: Hitler commits suicide.

May 8: Germany surrenders.

1957

Soviets report that Wallenberg died in prison July 16, 1947.

Chapter Notes

Chapter 1. Daring Rescue

1. John Bierman, *Righteous Gentile: The Story of Raoul Wallenberg, Missing Hero of the Holocaust* (New York: Viking Press, 1981), pp. 84–85. Reproduced by permission of Penguin Books, Ltd.

2. Kati Marton, *Wallenberg* (New York: Random House, 1982), p. 110.

3. Elenore Lester, *Wallenberg: The Man in the Iron Web* (Englewood Cliffs, N.J.: Prentice-Hall, 1982), p. 111.

4. Randolph L. Braham, *The Politics of Genocide: the Holocaust in Hungary, Condensed Edition* (Detroit: Wayne State University Press, 2000), Braham, p. 153.

5. Per Anger, *With Raoul Wallenberg in Budapest: Memories of the War Years in Hungary* (Washington, D.C.: Holocaust Library, 1996), p. 48.

6. Alan Gersten, *A Conspiracy of Indifference: the Raoul Wallenberg Story* (United States: XLibris, 2001), p. 53.

7. Frederick E. Werbell and Thurston Clarke, *Lost Hero: The Mystery of Raoul Wallenberg* (New York: McGraw-Hill, 1982), p. 104.

8. Gersten, p. 54.

9. Ibid.

10. Ibid.

11. Marton, p. 111.

12. Bierman, p. 82.

13. Anger, p. 83.

14. Bierman, p. 90.

Chapter 2. Unlikely Hero

1. John Bierman, *Righteous Gentile: The Story of Raoul Wallenberg, Missing Hero of the Holocaust* (New York: Viking Press, 1981), p. 20. Reproduced by permission of Penguin Books, Ltd.

2. Gustav Wallenberg, Letter to Raoul Wallenberg, dated Istanbul, September 8, 1932. In Raoul Wallenberg, *Letters and Dispatches, 1924–1944* (New York: Arcade Publishing, 1995), p. 78.

3. Yehuda Bauer, *A History of the Holocaust* (New York: Franklin Watts, 1982), p. 297.

4. Raoul Wallenberg, Letter to Gustav Wallenberg, dated Haifa, June 19, 1936, *Letters and Dispatches, 1924–1944*, p. 182.

5. Elenore Lester, *Wallenberg: The Man in the Iron Web* (Englewood Cliffs, N.J.: Prentice-Hall, 1982), p. 29.

6. Bierman, p. 25.

7. Raoul Wallenberg, Letter to Gustav Wallenberg, dated Haifa, July 6, 1936, *Letters and Dispatches, 1924–1944*, pp.186–187.

8. Frederick E. Werbell and Thurston Clarke, *Lost Hero: The Mystery of Raoul Wallenberg* (New York: McGraw-Hill, 1982), p. 22.

9. Lester, p. 53.

10. Bauer, pp. 300–301.

11. Ibid., p. 301.

12. Bierman, p. 12.

13. Ibid.

14. Hans Munch, "The Auschwitz Declaration," *Jewish Virtual Library*, 2003, <http://www.us-israel.org/jsource/Holocaust/audec.html> (July 13, 2003).

15. Randolph L. Braham, "The Holocaust in Hungary: A Retrospective Analysis," Randolph L Braham, ed., *The Nazis' Last Victims: The Holocaust in Hungary* (Detroit, Mich.: Wayne State University Press, 1998), pp. 35–36.

16. Randolph L. Braham, *The Politics of Genocide: The Holocaust in Hungary, Condensed Edition* (Detroit: Wayne State University Press, 2000, pp. 55–57.

17. Bierman, pp. 14–15.

18. PBS Online, "People and Events: Adolf Eichmann," *American Experience*, 1999, <http://www.pbs.org/wgbh/amex/holocaust/peopleevents/pandeAMEX86.html> (August 1, 2003).

19. Kati Marton, *Wallenberg* (New York: Random House, 1982), p. 58.

20. Jewish Virtual Library, "Adolf Eichmann," n.d., <http://www.us-israel.org/jsource/Holocaust/eichmann.html> (August 1, 2003).

21. Braham, *The Politics of Genocide*, 227.

22. Rudolf Vrba, "Preparations for the Holocaust in Hungary: An Eyewitness Account," Randolph L Braham, ed., *The Nazis' Last Victims*, p. 79.

23. Ibid., p. 68.

24. Bierman, p. 49.

25. Braham, *The Politics of Genocide*, p. 202.

Chapter 3. A Chance to Save Lives

1. Tony Kushner, "The Meaning of Auschwitz: Anglo-American Responses to the Hungarian Jewish Tragedy," in David Cesarani, *Genocide and Rescue: The Holocaust in Hungary 1944* (New York: Oxford, 1997), p. 172.

2. Beth Weiss, "The 'Blood for Trucks' Deal," *Jewish Virtual Library*, 2003. <http://www.us-israel.org/jsource/Holocaust/blood goods.html> (July 13, 2003).

3. Ibid.

4. John Bierman, *Righteous Gentile: The Story of Raoul Wallenberg, Missing Hero of the Holocaust* (New York: Viking Press, 1981), pp. 30–31. Reproduced by permission of Penguin Books, Ltd.

5. Elenore Lester, *Wallenberg: The Man in the Iron Web* (Englewood Cliffs, N.J.: Prentice-Hall, 1982), pp. 61–62.

6. Frederick E. Werbell and Thurston Clarke, *Lost Hero: The Mystery of Raoul Wallenberg* (New York: McGraw-Hill, 1982), p. 12.

7. Bierman, p. 36.

8. Ibid., p. 39.

9. Robert Rozett, "International Intervention: The Role of Diplomats in Attempts to Rescue Jews in Hungary," Randolph L Braham, ed., *The Nazis' Last Victims: The Holocaust in Hungary* (Detroit, Mich.: Wayne State University Press, 1998), p. 139.

10. Werbell and Clarke, p. 25.

11. Kati Marton, *Wallenberg* (New York: Random House, 1982), p. 45.

12. Per Anger, *With Raoul Wallenberg in Budapest: Memories of the War Years in Hungary* (Washington, D.C.: Holocaust Library, 1996), p. 38.

13. Rozett, p. 141.

14. Anger, p. 26.

15. Bierman, p. 52.

16. Raoul Wallenberg, *Letters and Dispatches, 1924–1944* (New York: Arcade Publishing, 1995), p. 229.

17. Ibid., p. 232.

18. Randolph L. Braham, *The Politics of Genocide: the Holocaust in Hungary, Condensed Edition* (Detroit: Wayne State University Press, 2000), p. 165.

19. Ibid., pp. 165–166.

20. Werbell and Clarke, p. 39.

21. Wallenberg, Letter to Maj von Dardel, dated Budapest, July 16, 1944, p. 273.

Chapter 4. Hope for the Jews

1. Rachel Oestreicher Bernheim, "A Hero for Our Time," *The Raoul Wallenberg Committee of the United States*, 2003, <http://www.raoulwallenberg.org/who/hero.html> (August 7, 2003).

2. Raoul Wallenberg, Letter to Maj von Dardel, dated Budapest, August 6, 1944, *Letters and Dispatches, 1924–1944* (New York: Arcade Publishing, 1995), p. 273.

3. Elenore Lester, *Wallenberg: The Man in the Iron Web* (Englewood Cliffs, N.J.: Prentice-Hall, 1982), p. 91.

4. Danny Smith, *Wallenberg: Lost Hero* (Springfield, Ill.: Templegate, 1986), p. 77.

5. Robert Rozett, "International Intervention: The Role of Diplomats in Attempts to Rescue Jews in Hungary," in Randolph L Braham, ed., *The Nazis' Last Victims: The Holocaust in Hungary* (Detroit: Wayne State University Press, 1998), p. 142.

6. Ibid.

7. Lester, pp. 94–95.

8. Ibid., p. 93.

9. Frederick E. Werbell and Thurston Clarke, *Lost Hero: The Mystery of Raoul Wallenberg* (New York: McGraw-Hill, 1982), p. 80.

10. Adam LeBor, *Hitler's Secret Bankers: The Myth of Swiss Neutrality* (Secaucus, NJ: Birch Lane Press, 1997), p. 187.

11. Tovia Preschel, Carl Lutz: "The Unsung Hero of Budapest's Jews," 1994. Online. http://www.cnwl.igs.net/~zes/unsung1.htm (Retrieved August 1, 2003).

12. Werbell and Clarke, pp. 50–52.

13. John Bierman, *Righteous Gentile: The Story of Raoul Wallenberg, Missing Hero of the Holocaust* (New York: Viking Press, 1981), p. 60. Reproduced by permission of Penguin Books, Ltd.

14. Lester, p. 98.

15. Werbell and Clarke, p. 49.

16. Andrew Handler, *A Man for All Connections: Raoul Wallenberg and the Hungarian State Apparatus, 1944–1945* (Westport, Conn.: Praeger, 1996), p. 63.

17. Ibid., p. 64.

Chapter 5. Power Struggle

1. Andrew Handler, *A Man for All Connections: Raoul Wallenberg and the Hungarian State Apparatus, 1944–1945* (Westport, Conn.: Praeger, 1996), p. 66.

2. Raoul Wallenberg, Letter to Maj von Dardel, dated Budapest, September 29, 1944, *Letters and Dispatches, 1924–1944* (New York: Arcade Publishing, 1995), p. 274.

3. Raoul Wallenberg, Dispatch dated September 12, 1944, *Letters and Dispatches, 1924–1944*, pp. 254–255.

4. Andrew Handler, *The Holocaust in Hungary: An Anthology of Jewish Response* (University, Ala.: University of Alabama Press, 1982), p. 24.

5. Handler, *A Man for All Connections*, p. 66.

6. Raoul Wallenberg, Dispatch dated September 29, 1944, *Letters and Dispatches, 1924–1944*, p. 256.

7. Frederick E. Werbell and Thurston Clarke, *Lost Hero: The Mystery of Raoul Wallenberg* (New York: McGraw-Hill, 1982), p. 59.

8. Kati Marton, *Wallenberg* (New York: Random House, 1982), p. 87.

9. Laura-Louise Veress, *Clear the Line: Hungary's Struggle to leave the Axis During the Second World War*, Corvinus Library, p. 280, <http://www.hungarian-history.hu/lib/clear/clear.pdf> (November 30, 2003).

10. Robert Rozett, "Jewish Armed Resistance in Hungary: A Comparative View," in *Genocide and Rescue: The Holocaust in Hungary 1944*, ed. David Cessarani (New York: Oxford, 1997), p. 138.

11. Raoul Wallenberg, Dispatch dated September 29, 1944, *Letters and Dispatches, 1924–1944*, p. 257.

12. Randolph L. Braham, *The Politics of Genocide: The Holocaust in Hungary* (Detroit: Wayne State University Press, 2000), p. 190.

13. Raoul Wallenberg, Dispatch dated September 29, 1944, *Letters and Dispatches, 1924–1944*, p. 258.

14. Robert Rozett, "International Intervention: The Role of Diplomats in Attempts to Rescue Jews in Hungary" in *The Nazis' Last Victims: The Holocaust in Hungary*, ed. Randolph Braham (Detroit, Mich.: Wayne State University Press), p. 143.

15. Braham, p. 51.

16. Werbell and Clarke, p. 55.

17. Handler, *A Man for All Connections*, p. 73.

18. Veress, pp. 280–281.

19. Hungary.Network, "The Policies of Prime Minister Kallay and the German Occupation of Hungary in March 1944," *Corvinus Library: Hungarian History*, 1999, n.d., <http://hungary.com/corvinus/index.htm> (August 26, 2003).

20. Veress, pp. 279, 281.

21. Jon Marmon, "Against All Odds," *Columns: The University of Washington Alumni Magazine*, September 1999, <http://www.washington.edu/alumni/columns/sept99/lantos2.html> (July 31, 2003).

22. Tom Lantos, speech accepting the Friend of Israel Award at Stand for Israel Washington Briefing Dinner, April 2, 2003, <http://206.67.54.108/sfi/downloads/TomLantos.pdf> (July 31, 2003).

23. Harvey Rosenfeld, *Raoul Wallenberg*, Revised ed. (New York: Holmes and Meier, 1995), p. 47.

Chapter 6. The Nyilas Nightmare Begins

1. Laura-Louise Veress, *Clear the Line: Hungary's Struggle to leave the Axis During the Second World War*, Corvinus Library, p. 295, <http://www.hungary-history.hu/corvinus/lib/clear/clear.pdf> (November 30, 2003).

2. Frederick E. Werbell and Thurston Clarke, *Lost Hero: The Mystery of Raoul Wallenberg* (New York: McGraw-Hill, 1982), p. 59–60.

3. Elenore Lester, *Wallenberg: The Man in the Iron Web* (Englewood Cliffs, N.J.: Prentice-Hall, 1982), p. 104.

4. Kati Marton, *Wallenberg* (New York: Random House, 1982), p. 92.

5. Veress, p. 293.

6. Randolph L. Braham, *The Politics of Genocide: The Holocaust in Hungary* (Detroit: Wayne State University Press, 2000), p. 184.

7. Lester, p. 105.

8. Harvey Rosenfeld, *Raoul Wallenberg*, Revised ed. (New York: Holmes and Meier, 1995), p. 87.

9. Danny Smith, *Wallenberg: Lost Hero* (Springfield, Ill.: Templegate, 1986), pp. 86–87.

10. Andrew Handler, *A Man for All Connections: Raoul Wallenberg and the Hungarian State Apparatus, 1944–1945* (Westport, Conn.: Praeger, 1996), p. 87.

11. Werbell and Clarke, p. 70.

12. Ibid.

13. Lester, p. 106.

14. John Bierman, *Righteous Gentile: The Story of Raoul Wallenberg, Missing Hero of the Holocaust* (New York: Viking Press, 1981), pp. 77–78. Reproduced by permission of Penguin Books, Ltd.

15. Marton, p. 227.

16. Werbell and Clarke, p. 77.

17. Braham, p. 186.

18. Handler, p. 94.

19. Yossi Klein Halevi, "The Troublemaker," *The Jerusalem Report.com*, 1999, <http://www.jrep.com/Info/10thAnniversary/1999/Article-9.html> (September 23, 2003).

20. John Bierman, *Righteous Gentile: The Story of Raoul Wallenberg, Missing Hero of the Holocaust* (New York: Viking Press, 1981), p. 89.

21. Handler, p. 90.

22. Raoul Wallenberg, Letter to Maj von Dardel, dated Budapest, October 22, 1944, *Letters and Dispatches, 1924–1944* (New York: Arcade Publishing, 1995), p. 276.

23. Raoul Wallenberg, Dispatch dated October 22, 1944, *Letters and Dispatches, 1924–1944*, p. 263.

Chapter 7. Marched to Death

1. Elenore Lester, *Wallenberg: The Man in the Iron Web* (Englewood Cliffs, N.J.: Prentice-Hall, 1982), p. 112.

2. Frederick E. Werbell and Thurston Clarke, *Lost Hero: The Mystery of Raoul Wallenberg* (New York: McGraw-Hill, 1982), p. 81.

3. Ibid., pp. 83–84.

4. Randolph L. Braham, *The Politics of Genocide: The Holocaust in Hungary* (Detroit: Wayne State University Press, 2000), pp. 187–188.

5. Harvey Rosenfeld, *Raoul Wallenberg*, Revised ed. (New York: Holmes and Meier, 1995), p. 50.

6. Werbell and Clarke, p. 89.

7. Lester, p. 110.

8. Danny Smith, *Wallenberg: Lost Hero* (Springfield, Ill.: Templegate, 1986), p. 95.

9. Rosenfeld, p. 58.

10. Kati Marton, *Wallenberg* (New York: Random House, 1982), pp. 109–110.

11. Lester, p. 109.

12. Per Anger, *With Raoul Wallenberg in Budapest: Memories of the War Years in Hungary* (Washington, D.C.: Holocaust Library, 1996), p. 58.

13. John Bierman, *Righteous Gentile: The Story of Raoul Wallenberg, Missing Hero of the Holocaust* (New York: Viking Press, 1981), p. 83. Reproduced by permission of Penguin Books, Ltd.

14. Ibid., pp. 83–84.

15. Smith, p. 100.

16. Ibid., p. 93.

17. Rosenfeld, p. 85.

18. Andrew Handler, *A Man for All Connections: Raoul Wallenberg and the Hungarian State Apparatus, 1944–1945* (Westport, Conn.: Praeger, 1996), p. 95.

19. Werbell and Clarke, p. 94.

20. Tom Veres, "I Was There," *Beliefnet*, 2003, <http://www.belief net.com/frameset.asp?boardID=14824&pageloc=/story/75/story_7559_ 1.html> (July 30, 2003).

21. Ibid.

22. Braham, p. 220.

23. Bierman, p. 81.

24. Werbell and Clarke, p. 107.

25. Eugene Lebovitz and Kate Lebovitz, personal interview, October 21, 2003.

26. Ibid.

27. Braham, p. 190.

28. Rosenfeld, p. 62.

29. Ibid., pp. 62–63.

30. Eleonore Lappin, "The Death Marches of Hungarian Jews Through Austria in the Spring of 1945," *Yad Vashem Studies*, p. 8, 2004, <http://www.yadvashem.org/download/about_holocaust/studies/ lappin_full.pdf> (April 13, 2004).

31. Marton, pp. 109–110.

32. Werbell and Clarke, p. 108.

33. Ibid.

Chapter 8. Unholy Nights

1. Frederick E. Werbell and Thurston Clarke, *Lost Hero: The Mystery of Raoul Wallenberg* (New York: McGraw-Hill, 1982), p. 114.

2. Ibid.

3. Raoul Wallenberg, Dispatch dated December 12, 1944, *Letters and Dispatches, 1924–1944* (New York: Arcade Publishing, 1995), p. 267.

4. Randolph L. Braham, *The Politics of Genocide: The Holocaust in Hungary* (Detroit: Wayne State University Press, 2000), p. 191.

5. Harvey Rosenfeld, *Raoul Wallenberg*, Revised ed. (New York: Holmes and Meier, 1995), p. 64.

6. Werbell and Clarke, p. 115.

7. Laura-Louise Veress, *Clear the Line: Hungary's Struggle to leave the Axis During the Second World War*, Corvinus Library, p. 304, <http://www.hungary-history.hu/corvinus/lib/clear/clear.pdf> (November 30, 2003).

8. Braham, p. 194.

9. Kati Marton, *Wallenberg* (New York: Random House, 1982), pp. 123–124.

10. Braham, pp. 194–195.

11. Kate Lebovitz, personal interview, October 21, 2003.

12. Rosenfeld, p. 68.

13. Kate Lebovitz, personal interview, October 21, 2003.

14. Raoul Wallenberg, Dispatch dated December 12, 1944, *Letters and Dispatches, 1924–1944*, pp. 265–266.

15. Per Anger, *With Raoul Wallenberg in Budapest: Memories of the War Years in Hungary* (Washington, D.C.: Holocaust Library, 1996), pp. 63–67.

16. Anger, p. 97.

17. Danny Smith, *Wallenberg: Lost Hero* (Springfield, Ill.: Templegate, 1986), p. 107.

18. Werbell and Clarke, p. 118.

19. Anger, p. 65.

20. Werbell and Clarke, p. 127.

21. Marton, p. 134.

22. Anger, p. 67.

23. Frederick E. Werbell and Thurston Clarke, *Lost Hero: The Mystery of Raoul Wallenberg* (New York: McGraw-Hill, 1982), p. 142.

24. Agnes Mandl Adachi, "Rescue: Personal Stories," *United States Holocaust Memorial Museum*, 1992, <http://www.ushmm.org/wlc/en/> (August 2, 2003).

25. Anger, p. 73.

26. John Bierman, *Righteous Gentile: The Story of Raoul Wallenberg, Missing Hero of the Holocaust* (New York: Viking Press, 1981), p. 106. Reproduced by permission of Penguin Books, Ltd.

27. Elenore Lester, *Wallenberg: The Man in the Iron Web* (Englewood Cliffs, N.J.: Prentice-Hall, 1982), pp. 122–123.

28. Bierman, p. 110.

29. Rosenfeld, p. 94.

30. Werbell and Clarke, p. 135.

31. Bierman, p. 96.

32. Ibid.

33. Anger, p. 75.

34. Werbell and Clarke, p. 131.

35. Ibid., p. 128.

36. Otto Komoly, "What May Jews Learn from the Present Crisis?" in Andrew Handler, ed., *The Holocaust in Hungary: An Anthology of Jewish Response* (University, Ala.: University of Alabama Press, 1982), pp. 48–52.

37. Robert Rozett, "Otto Komoly," in *Encyclopedia of the Holocaust, Vol. 2* (New York: MacMillan Publishing Co., 1990), p. 815.

38. Randolph L. Braham, *The Politics of Genocide: The Holocaust in Hungary, Condensed Edition* (Detroit: Wayne State University Press, 2000), p. 192.

39. Rozett, p. 815.

40. Rosenfeld, p. 68.

Chapter 9. Liberation and Imprisonment

1. Elenore Lester, *Wallenberg: The Man in the Iron Web* (Englewood Cliffs, N.J.: Prentice-Hall, 1982), pp. 124–125.

2. John Bierman, *Righteous Gentile: The Story of Raoul Wallenberg, Missing Hero of the Holocaust* (New York: Viking Press, 1981), p. 113. Reproduced by permission of Penguin Books, Ltd.

3. Kati Marton, *Wallenberg* (New York: Random House, 1982), p. 142.

4. Ibid., p. 140.

5. Frederick E. Werbell and Thurston Clarke, *Lost Hero: The Mystery of Raoul Wallenberg* (New York: McGraw-Hill, 1982), pp. 146–147.

6. Marton, pp. 142–143.

7. Danny Smith, *Wallenberg: Lost Hero* (Springfield, Ill.: Templegate, 1986), p. 117.

8. Marton, p. 146.

9. Marton, p. 153.

10. Lester, p. 31.

11. Werbell and Clarke, p. 153.

12. Marton, p. 152.

13. Bierman, p. 116.

14. Werbell and Clarke, p. 159.

15. Rosenfeld, p. 101.

16. Kate Lebovitz, personal interview, October 21, 2003.

17. Per Anger, *With Raoul Wallenberg in Budapest: Memories of the War Years in Hungary* (Washington, D.C.: Holocaust Library, 1996), pp. 100–104.

18. Anger, pp. 123–130.

19. "A Failure of Diplomacy," *Commission of Inquiry, Swedish Ministry of Foreign Affairs*, March 4, 2003, <http://www.utrikes. regeringen.se/inenglish/policy/wallenberg/pdf/wallenberg_en.pdf> (April 13, 2004).

20. Anger, p. 148.

21. *Commission of Inquiry*, p. 30.

22. Ibid., p. 32.

23. Ibid., p. 30.

24. Ibid., p. 31.

25. Ibid., p. 33.

26. Ibid., p. 35.

27. Rosenfeld, p. 121.

28. Smith, p. 140.

29. Anger, p. 159.

30. *Commission of Inquiry*, p. 40.

31. Smith, p. 138.

32. Rosenfeld, p. 123.

33. Marton, pp. 184–187.

34. Charles Fenyvesi and Victoria Pope, "The Angel was a Spy," *U.S. News and World Report*, May 13, 1996, p. 56.

35. "Russia Concedes a Point on Wallenberg's Fate," *New York Times*, July 26, 2000, p. A3.

36. "Russia Tells a Bit More About Wallenberg's Fate," *New York Times*, December 23, 2000, p. A10.

Chapter 10. Rescuer or Spy?

1. Iver C. Olsen, Letter to Brigadier General William O'Dwyer, dated June 15, 1945, *Letters and Dispatches, 1924–1944* (New York: Arcade Publishing, 1995), p. 269.

2. Kati Marton, *Wallenberg* (New York: Random House, 1982), p. 174.

3. Charles Fenyvesi and Victoria Pope, "The Angel was a Spy," *U.S. News and World Report*, May 13, 1996, p. 51.

4. Ibid., p. 53.

5. Per Anger, *With Raoul Wallenberg in Budapest: Memories of the War Years in Hungary* (Washington, D.C.: Holocaust Library, 1996), p. 168.

6. Randolph L. Braham, *The Politics of Genocide: The Holocaust in Hungary, Condensed Edition* (Detroit: Wayne State University Press, 2000), p. 252.

7. Olsen, p. 269.

8. Yehuda Bauer, "Conclusion: The Holocaust in Hungary: Was Rescue Possible?" in David Cesarani, *Genocide and Rescue: The Holocaust in Hungary 1944* (New York: Oxford, 1997), p. 205.

9. Braham, p. 252.

10. Frederick E. Werbell and Thurston Clarke, *Lost Hero: The Mystery of Raoul Wallenberg* (New York: McGraw-Hill, 1982), p. 159.

11. Olsen, p. 269.

12. Roll Call: 'The Righteous Among Nations' Diplomats," *Holocaust Survivors' Network*, "December 15, 2002, <http://isurvived.org/RollCall-4theRighteous_1.html> (November 30, 2003).

13. Kate Lebovitz, personal interview, October 21, 2003.

14. Ibid.

15. Ibid.

16. "The Righteous Among the Nations—Statistics and Stories," *Yad Vashem, The Holocaust Martyrs' and Heroes' Remembrance Authority*, n.d., <http://www.yadvashem.org/righteous/index_righteous.html> (November 30, 2003).

17. "Online Exhibitions: Visas for Life: Diplomats that Rescued Jews," *Yad Vashem, The Holocaust Martyrs' and Heroes' Remembrance Authority*, n.d., <http://www.yadvashem.org/exhibitions/index_exhibitions.html> (July 20, 2004).

18. Eugene Lebovitz and Kate Lebovitz, personal interview, October 21, 2003.

19. Allen Lebovitz, personal interview, October 21, 2003.

Glossary

Allies—Nations that joined together to fight against Hitler's Germany and the other Axis nations. In 1944–1945, the Allies included Britain, the United States, the Soviet Union, and others.

anti-Semite—Person who displays hatred toward Jews (anti-Semitism).

Arrow Cross—Pro-Nazi members of Ferenc Szálasi's Nyilas party.

Axis—Nations fighting on the German side in World War II.

consul—Government official who looks after the business and citizens of his or her country in a foreign land.

crematorium—A building containing ovens used to burn bodies to ashes.

death marches—Program to transport Jews from one place to another by forcing them to walk great distances under conditions that many could not survive.

deportation—The transport of a person out of a country.

Fascism—Political philosophy such as Nazism that places the government as first priority over individual freedom. Usually includes dictatorship and racist policies.

Final Solution—Euphemism used in Nazi communication to indicate programs to kill Jews.

Führer—German leader. Adolf Hitler's title.

gendarmes—Armed police or militia.

genocide—The systematic killing of a racial or ethnic group.

Gentile—Non-Jewish person.

gestapo—The Nazi Secret State Police. The name is a shortened version of the German name Geheime Staats Polizei.

ghetto—An area in which people of a certain ethnic group live. Jews were forced to live within restricted areas in many parts of Europe during World War II.

gulag—Soviet prison system.

halutzim—Yiddish word meaning "pioneers." It was the name of a secret youth resistance group that worked to save Jews from the Nazis.

Jewish Joint Distribution Committee—Also American Jewish Joint Distribution Committee. An American organization formed to collect money to be used to help Jews.

Jewish Star—Six-pointed Star of David, symbol of Jewish faith. Yellow stars were used to identify Jewish people and houses.

Judaism—The Jewish faith.

Judenrein—Yiddish word for a place from which all Jews have been removed.

kommando—Labor squads made up of concentration camp prisoners.

legation—A diplomatic office and its staff in a foreign land.

Magyar—A person of mainstream Hungarian culture. Jews who identified more with Hungarian culture than Jewish culture were said to be "Magyarized."

NKVD—Soviet secret police.

Nyilas party—Ferenc Szálasi's pro-Nazi political party which overthrew the Hungarian government of Miklós Horthy on October 15, 1944. Commonly referred to as the Arrow Cross Party.

OSS—Office of Strategic Services. The American agency for gathering international intelligence. Later was changed to Central Intelligence Agency (CIA).

plenipotentiary—A diplomat with full authority to represent his government in a foreign country. German Edmund Veesenmayer was given this title and power in Hungary.

pogrom—An organized massacre.

Schutz-pass—(Also Schütz-passe) Protective pass given by Swedish and Swiss legations to Jews in Hungary. Certified them as Swedish or Swiss citizens, eligible for emigration to that country.

SMERSH—Soviet foreign intelligence agency. In Russian means "Kill the spies!"

sonderkommando—Special squad. The SS unit commanded by Adolf Eichmann in charge of carrying out the Final Solution in Hungary. The term is also used to refer to Jewish labor units in concentration camps that took dead bodies from the gas chambers to the crematoria.

SS—Abbreviation for Schutzstaffel or Protection Squad. Hitler's elite military squad that pledged absolute obedience to him. Carried out mass executions of Jews.

Third Reich—Meaning "third regime or empire." The title given to Hitler's Germany and its government. The medieval Holy Roman Empire until 1806 was considered the First Reich. The German Empire from 1871–1918 was considered the Second Reich.

153

WRB—War Refugee Board. A committee formed by President Franklin Roosevelt in January 1944 to aid Holocaust victims, after the meaning of "Final Solution" was discovered.

yellow-star houses—Houses marked by banners displaying the Jewish Star of David, used to identify houses in which Jews lived.

Zionist—Movement for (or person in favor of) establishment of a Jewish homeland in Palestine.

Zyklon-B—Hydrogen cyanide, a deadly chemical gas used in the extermination chambers at Auschwitz.

Further Reading

By Wallenberg:

Wallenberg, Raoul. *Letters and Dispatches 1924–1944*. New York: Arcade Publishing, 1995.

Books about Wallenberg:

Bierman, John. *Righteous Gentile: The Story of Raoul Wallenberg, Missing Hero of the Holocaust*. New York: Viking Press, 1981.

Lester, Elenore. *Wallenberg: The Man in the Iron Web*. Englewood Cliffs, N.J.: Prentice-Hall, 1982.

Marton, Kati. *Wallenberg*. New York: Random House, 1982.

Werbell, Frederick and Thurston Clarke. *Lost Hero: The Mystery of Raoul Wallenberg*. New York: McGraw-Hill, 1982.

Books about other rescuers:

Lyman, David. *Holocaust Rescuers: Ten Stories of Courage*. Berkeley Heights, N.J.: Enslow Publishers, Inc., 1999.

Skoglund, Elizabeth. *A Quiet Courage: Per Anger, Wallenberg's Co-liberator of Hungarian Jews*. Grand Rapids, Mich.: Baker Books, 1997.

Tschuy, Theo. *Dangerous diplomacy: the story of Carl Lutz: Rescuer of 62,000 Hungarian Jews*. Grand Rapids, Mich.: William B. Eerdmans, 2000.

Personal Stories of the Hungarian Holocaust:

Anger, Per. *With Raoul Wallenberg in Budapest: Memories of the War Years in Hungary*. Washington, D.C.: Holocaust Library, 1996.

Grove, Andrew S. *Swimming Across: A Memoir*. New York: Warner Books, 2001.

Jackson, Livia Bitton. *I Have Lived a Thousand Years: Growing up in the Holocaust*. New York: Simon & Schuster Books for Young Readers, 1997.

Rosner, Bernat. *An Uncommon Friendship: From Opposite Sides of the Holocaust*. Berkeley: University of California Press, 2001.

Soros, Tivador. *Masquerade: Dancing Around Death in Nazi-Occupied Hungary*. New York: Arcade Publishing, 2001.

Video Recordings:

McCullough, David G. WGBH Boston. *America and the Holocaust: Deceit and Indifference.* Alexandria, Va.: PBS Video, 1994.

Spielberg, Steven and The Shoah Foundation. *The Last Days.* New York: Polygram Video, 1998.

Magazine Articles:

Elliot, L. "The Haunting Riddle of Raoul Wallenberg." *Reader's Digest,* January 1991, pp. 114–119.

Fenyvesi, Charles. "New Clue." *U.S. News and World Report,* July 11, 1994, p. 24.

Fenyvesi, Charles and Victoria Pope, "The Angel was a Spy," *U.S. News and World Report,* May 13, 1996, pp. 46–57.

Hood, R. E. "The Missing Hero." *Boys' Life.* April 1992, pp. 22–26.

Korey, William. "Wallenberg and the Undelivered Letter." *Christian Science Monitor,* August 28, 1995, p. 19.

_____. "The Case of Raoul Wallenberg." *Freedom Review,* August 1994, pp. 41–42.

Newspaper Articles:

"Russia Concedes a Point on Wallenberg's Fate," *New York Times,* July 26, 2000, p. A3.

"Russia Tells a Bit More About Wallenberg's Fate," *New York Times,* December 23, 2000, p. A10.

Internet Addresses

"Raoul Wallenberg." *Jewish Virtual Library.* 2004.
<http://www.jewishvirtuallibrary.org>

Click on "Enter the Library," then on "Biography," then on "Raoul Wallenberg." Provides biographical information. Also includes link to the Jewish Virtual Library's searchable home page.

Bernheim, Rachel Oestreicher.
"A Hero for Our Time."
The Raoul Wallenberg Committee of the United States. 2003.
<http://www.raoulwallenberg.org>

Click "Enter Site." Click "Who Is Raoul Wallenberg?" at top of page. Then click "A Hero for Our Time." Includes photos by Tom Veres and links to related sites.

Simon Weisenthal Center.
Museum of Tolerance Multimedia Learning Center Online. 1997.
<http://motlc.wiesenthal.com>

Click on "Multimedia Learning Center." Virtual Holocaust encyclopedia with thousands of text files and photographs.

Index

158